THE HUMAN ESSENCE OF ECONOMICS

The Human Essence of Economics

A Microeconomic Textbook Alternative

Divine Microeconomy
A Tapestry of Human Virtues

BRUCE KOERBER

10 9 8 7 6 5 4 3 2

ISBN: 978-0-9960955-6-3 (print)
ISBN: 978-0-9960955-1-8 (ebook)

OL25808992M

Dedicated to my classical liberalism lineage, which is as follows:

– Roger Garrison

– back to Murray N. Rothbard

– back to Ludwig von Mises

– back to Eugen von Böhm-Bawerk

and back to Carl Menger, who rekindled classical liberalism with the publication in 1871 of

Principles of Economics[7]

"There cannot be too much of a correct theory."
—Ludwig von Mises

Contents

Acknowledgement

In the interim between 2006 when I published *DIVINE MICROECONOMY: A Tapestry of Human Virtues* and the present I became aware of a book written by Milton Shapiro. It came to my attention when I was browsing on the Mises Institute website where it was very highly recommended as a book about microeconomics from an Austrian economics perspective.

Dr. Milton Shapiro considers himself a devoted student of Mises, who he says 'humanized economics.' Inspired by *Human Action* and other works of Ludwig von Mises Milton Shapiro wrote *Foundations of the Market Price System*.

I found myself greatly impressed with this book written by Dr. Shapiro, who taught economics at California State Polytechnic University, Pomona, for 25 years. After corresponding and speaking with Dr. Shapiro he agreed to allow me to acknowledge my indebtedness to the clarity and precision of his insights put forth in his book.

Part of my indebtedness to Dr. Shapiro is due to the information conveyed in the diagrams found in *Foundations of the Market Price System* which I modified and used in Chapter 3 to help me to describe the core economic concepts. These include Diagrams 3b, 3c, 3d, 3e, 3f, 3g and 3h and Table 3a.

Foreword

This is a book about economics. It includes the expected discussion of topics such as supply and demand, profit and loss, and market-clearing price. It also includes charts and graphs, but disaffected students of economics will be relieved to know that those are easy to understand and relatively sparse.

But this is much more than an economics book. It is fashionable in our contemporary culture to adopt a philosophical approach of pure materialism/empiricism. Whether the field is physics, evidence-based medicine, or economics, one begins with the ideas that 1) everything that happens can be explained by the interaction of matter and energy, and 2) that only results that can be directly observed and measured are meaningful. Bruce Koerber understands that embracing these ideas leads to restricted, incomplete, and sometimes misleading interpretation of results. Instead he approaches economics much as the pioneers of the physical sciences did in the 1600s.

Researchers such as Kepler, Boyle, and Newton discerned that there was a certain order to the universe. They sought to discover and understand the principles by which it operates. They did not view this natural order as accidental, but reflective of the system's Designer. Without this conviction that orderly principles exist, they would have had no reason to undertake the search that led to the discovery of important laws of physics and chemistry.

The author of this book begins with the premise that human beings are more than just material entities. Human nature includes a spark of the divine and therefore reflects—albeit in an incomplete and broken way—the divine nature. This human image of the divine gives mankind goals and wants beyond material needs, pleasure, and pain. We humans are cognizant of the past, have aspirations for the future, and understand that posterity will transcend our own lifetimes. We contemplate concepts of order, justice, cooperation, love, charity, and mercy. And while we share certain experiences, we each have our subjective consciousness which distinguishes us as individuals.

The discussion acknowledges that the economy comprises the decisions of a multitude of individuals, each one motivated by material needs but also by goals and values that transcend the material. The Divine Economy results when these individuals interact according to their own desires and needs, but also in pursuit of goals such as unity, compassion, and justice. Since individuals act subjectively, the economy is never completely predictable and never static. It seeks equilibrium without achieving it. This dynamism, as the root word implies, provides the energy that the economy needs to adapt.

This type of analysis also clarifies why it is folly to attempt to "manage" the economy in a meaningful way through central planning. The decisions of bureaucrats, no matter how selfless or well intentioned, cannot replace nor meet the individual goals of thousands of people. Attempts to change the inherent principles of the economy produce distortions of commerce in the short run, and ultimately fail. When the economy is allowed to operate according to its divinely-inspired principles, it can thrive.

Read this book thoughtfully, not to amass facts, but to appreciate its principles. Perhaps reflection on the Divine Economy Model will lead to new understanding of your own goals. And you will see that the economy is designed to serve both temporal and eternal purposes.

Donald Nelson, MD
Cedar Rapids, Iowa

List of Figures

List of Figures

Introduction:
A Fine Gift!

Receiving It Graciously!

PREFACE

Wise travelers from a distant time and place find themselves mesmerized by the arrival of a long awaited event. Before they set out on their journey they devote all of their resources to the long trip and to capturing the exquisite simplicity of the honored gift. Traversing the sands of time and moving perceptively nearer and nearer to their destination a feeling of exhilaration and exaltation seizes the bearers of this priceless gift. After much sacrifice and toil the travelers finally approach the vicinity of the consummation of the consecrated task. At the threshold of the exchange all the surroundings are electrified with indescribable joy and wonder. A fine gift is presented and graciously received.

THE GIFT OF THE ECONOMY!

The wrapped gift is received. Do we really see it or are certain things hidden from our sight? Frankly, even if we gaze upon it we still may be unable to fully perceive what it is that is in front of us.

Blindfolded, or not, I can hold the gift in my hands and still not know what it is. Its surface may have a certain texture detectable to the touch. Whatever it is it has a certain weight to it. Even without a blindfold there is only so much I can be sure of, such as the color of the fabric that is wrapped around the object that is inside.

With all of our faculties fully available to us it is still a mystery. The economy is like this gift, wrapped in a fine and exquisite tapestry.

The gift is the whole thing: the beautiful covering and the undiscovered object of great value still concealed. These two parts of the gift are inseparable just like the economy is inseparable from that which makes it appear in the world—all the human beings in the world—like you and me.

Full appreciation of the gift comes from enjoying its wholeness without others imposing expectations on us. Those expectations would diminish the whole experience. What expectations have been tacked onto the economy, diminishing its value to us? We are told and expected to believe that the economy causes us to behave in certain ways, for example, some suppose that the economy beckons us to become rich and to bowl over others to achieve that goal.

This is the reverse of what is the true reality of the economy. Sure, we see such things happening in this manner but it is ultimately because the ego-driven interventionists are using the economy to benefit themselves. What we are seeing is this: we are seeing what the economy looks like when it is in a corrupted state, and like it or not we happen to be living in a time such as this. Correcting this error can be considered as our great challenge.

The Gracious Economy!

In truth the economy is a reflection of human cooperation. It is that and more. The economy has the potential to reflect all of the inherent qualities of mutuality and reciprocity residing in humankind. The economy exists because human beings exist. Its potential is their potential! "Acting and thinking man is the product of a universe of scarcity in which whatever well-being can be attained is the prize of toil and trouble, of conduct popularly called economic."[12, p. 236]

The economy is whole. And there is no separation within it. Those who try to carve it up are interventionists and their acts corrupt the economy. We see nations trying to carve out their piece of the economy, acting like mercantilists and ignorant of the destructive nature of their actions. How then can we expect a corrupted economy to bring about prosperity?

It is our great challenge and our responsibility to dispel this ignorance; and the reason we must do this is because it affects us very deeply, every day and everywhere. This omnipresent impact stems from the universal nature of the economy. Our permitting and tolerating of intervention affects ourselves, and it affects everyone.

What does it look like to have no intervention? Some see it as a free market economy. I see it as that and more. God created human beings and endowed them with His names and attributes. Using these, and developing these in conjunction and along with our fellow human beings, creates the sparks in time and place when there is the appearance of the economy in the world. Since the potential of human beings is divine—i.e., the possession of and manifesting of the attributes of God—so also necessarily is the economy.

It is the appearance of human virtues which acts like a lodestone. When a person exhibits truthfulness, all the relationships that depend on truthfulness—business and personal—are drawn to that person. It is the appearance of these virtues, and the attraction that they create, that bring about both justice and unity. These divine qualities that are inherent in human beings are ultimately the source of prosperity.

And it follows that taking notice is the key. First of all, taking notice is one of the defining characteristics of a human being. Humans take notice because they are always seeking: seeking what is best. Secondly, taking notice is an incredible power and a motivating force. It is what causes us to seek loyal friends, honest partners, creative teachers, etc.

This inherent drive is all about being alert. Seen in this way it is evident that even entrepreneurship is essentially an exercise of a part of our spiritual reality. Those who exhibit praiseworthy characteristics will be found. And it is the desirability of human virtues that will continually move human civilization towards prosperity.

For centuries we have tried to direct the economy. It is now time to recognize the economy as a divine institution that encourages human development and brings about prosperity. The other way—intervention —is divisive and its failure is all around us and is progressively worsening. This shortcoming is necessarily so because intervention causes a corruption of the divine economy.

At the most basic level what we are talking about is a spiritual solution of the economic problems. By definition, a 'foundation' is what everything rests upon. Void of the spiritual qualities—the attributes of God—what kind of foundation is the economy built upon? It is clear that now is the time to leave the outworn ideas of intervention behind because they offer no foundation and also because acts of intervention disrupt the flow of information and corrupt the potential of the divine economy.

In this book I find a logical starting point, despite the disparate views within economic circles. Next I build a model that allows you to be directly engaged in the process of the merging of science and religion. This will be a truly a remarkable experience for you since it is a brand new concept in the world, never done before, and you will be among the first to go there. Then I offer you, the reader, a strong economic foundation to counter the naysayers—and there will be naysayers!

Next, what follows in the book is a practical connection of theory, and of the model, and of how our economic life works, with examples that demonstrate how values originate. And finally I show that it is the entrepreneur who emerges, rising like a phoenix, as the one who activates all of the powers in the economy.

Chapter 1
What's Inside?

Is it a Gem?

PREFACE

The gift is wrapped and for this reason we do not know what is inside the wrappings of the beautiful tapestry. There really is only one way to satisfy our curiosity. Unless and until we faithfully unwrap the covering no amount of imagining will make it real. As soon as the contents are revealed by disrobing the gift, a whole new reality bares itself and everything changes.

In parallel how can it be regarded as satisfactory to have economic theory that does not fully encompass human nature or adequately serve humanity? Until there is such a comprehensive theory it can be said that economics still is in its infancy.

Until economic theory achieves that pinnacle it will continue to be inadequate and everyone will suffer. However, once that pinnacle is attained it will be like the monumental difference that occurred in medical science after the acceptance of germ theory compared with before. It's like knowing what is inside the wrapping.

WHERE DO WE GO FROM HERE?

Once that important threshold is reached, new vistas will open up. Try to imagine the difference! In economics it will be like the difference between being considered 'the dismal science' and being considered the science of human action—and even more monumental—being considered the science of purposeful action by spiritual beings! The excitement builds! What is inside?

Imagine the difference in your life and the life of your children when what will be understood as the source of prosperity for you and for everyone is the acquisition of noble traits. The economic ills associated with contrariness will disappear. Imagine the effect on business ethics and consider the high attainment of civilization when entrepreneurial alertness is directed towards refinement of human virtues. Maybe what is 'inside' us is just as much a mystery and just as much a gift!

Although at first it may seem like a contradictory objective, it is the goal of this book to look at the real world and its circumstances in order to gain an understanding of the divine microeconomy. The choice of this goal is motivated by the search for an understanding of the economy that is logically whole. Getting there will require an effort to either find a bridge or to build a bridge between the spiritual foundation of the human being and the economy, and then to show how that foundation manifests itself in the realm of action.

> "Acting man is always concerned both with "material" and "ideal" things. He chooses between various alternatives, no matter whether they are to be classified as material or ideal. In the actual scales of value material and ideal things are jumbled together. Even if it were feasible to draw a sharp line between material and ideal concerns, one must realize that every concrete action either aims at the realization both of material and ideal ends or is the outcome of a choice between something material and something ideal.
>
> Whether it is possible to separate neatly those actions which aim at the satisfaction of needs exclusively conditioned by man's physiological constitution from other "higher" needs can be left undecided. But we must not overlook the fact that in reality no food is valued solely for its nutritive power and no garment or house solely for the protection it affords against cold weather and rain. It cannot be denied that the demand for goods is widely influenced by metaphysical, religious, and ethical considerations, by aesthetic value judgments, by customs, habits, prejudices, tradition, changing fashions, and many other things. To an economist who would try to restrict his investigations to "material" aspects only, the subject matter of inquiry vanishes as soon as he wants to catch it."[12, pp. 233–4]

WHAT ARE THE BASICS?

To start we will consider demand theory which can be described more accurately by the designation 'consumer demand theory of value.' The reason this is an important clarification is because it identifies the consumer as the source of demand and indicates that it is the consumer who determines value. And since each human acts as a spokesperson for himself or herself it can be said that we make decisions subjectively.

It's decision time! When the time and place comes for a decision to be made it occurs at the margin, and it pertains specifically to a marginal unit. For example, an individual knows the value of an apple but is not concerned with the total value of all the apples in the world.

It is also true that each of us prioritizes our needs. If you are hungry, you will value an apple more than a pencil. This prioritizing is done ordinally not cardinally so, at the time and place of action, it matters not if the apple is twenty times or two times more valuable than the pencil—the apple is simply, subjectively, and ordinally preferred.

How do we do it? There are certain resources that serve as the means to be used towards the goal of achieving your ends. Economics is the "science of the means to be applied for the attainment of ends chosen."[12, p. 10] Humans like you and I take courses of action, using various means, which lead to an improved state of being. The applied science of economics pertains to productive efforts of any kind that are made to attain ends that seem to be within the realm of possibility.

What is the lingo? The scientific terminology that describes the operating power of the microeconomy is equilibrium and its tendency. That is what moves it! For example, the price system works like the governor of an engine. If the engine begins to run too fast the operating power of the governor slows the engine. The same moderating effect occurs if the engine is being bogged down and strained, with the governor accelerating it to bring it into balance. If the price for a good is too high the demand will lessen causing changes in the system until demand and supply are balanced.

Let it be stated that there is some compatibility between contemporary microeconomics and the new idea which is presented in this book. The new idea about to be introduced in this book is the divine microeconomy. But before I introduce more about the divine microeconomy I need to make sure that you understand that there are conflicting views in the economic literature and the economic profession about how to approach the subject of economics.

WHICH APPROACH TO TAKE?

The standard version is what is called the contemporary price theory, the version of microeconomics that adopts the neoclassical methodology of empiricism. It is the present day school of thought that follows a lineage of Adam Smith, then Ricardo, Mill, Marshall, and Chamberlain. It was out of this tradition that the idea to dissect the economy came from. The economy was separated and partitioned into different parts and subsequently into micro and macro.

The predominant characteristic of contemporary price theory is its empirical equilibrium analysis. Out of this approach sprung the labor theory of value and the familiar Chamberlainian models of perfect competition, imperfect competition, oligopoly and monopoly.

What is overlooked and forgotten is that these Chamberlainian models are built upon specific mental constructs. The starting point for all of these empirical models is the assumption of equilibrium. They are in the state of equilibrium. In other words, nothing is moving them away from where they are!

Consequently and ironically there is no competition for the consumers' choices in the 'perfect competition model' (no deviation from the practices of the other producers) since supply equals demand in this balanced state of equilibrium. In these models the entrepreneur is seen as a *profit maximizing decision-maker* which leads to the conclusion that the entrepreneur is *responsible for the appearance of a monopoly*. With all due respect these are two examples of the economic fallacies (italicized in the previous sentence) that stem directly from the use of the empirical methodology, a methodology which, frankly speaking, is not suited for economic science.

The alternative approach which evolved concurrently from different minds is the science of economics that developed within another lineage. That lineage is comprised of the Spanish Scholastics and the French and Continental economic thinkers—a branch of economic thought which is regarded as the classical liberalism tradition. In the mid to late 1800's there was a rekindling of this tradition. The lineage of this rejuvenated tradition extends to the present: beginning with Menger, continuing through Böhm-Bawerk, Mises and Kirzner; which brings this school of thought to the current microeconomic theory of classical liberalism — a theory best described as competitive entrepreneurship. [5]

The principal characteristic in competitive entrepreneurship is its analysis of the economy in disequilibrium since the economy is always in disequilibrium — tending toward equilibrium. In contrast to the neoclassical theory, the forces of equilibrium are unsettled and in disequilibrium and are always active, moving, and pressuring the economy. The application of the methodology of classical liberalism introduces the concept of subjectivism which then permits the study of economics to proceed as a qualitative science rather than a quantitative one. After all, economics is a philosophical science not a mathematical one.

You and I know what we value. The value scale that people use in real life is subjective. It reflects the subjective value of the marginal utility derived from each good and it reflects the ordinal (rather than cardinal) nature of value.

From this subjectivist perspective it is the entrepreneurs who are seen as the persons acting upon their awareness of price discrepancies within the economic system. The firm is seen as a combination of the entrepreneur and the resource owner. From this perspective it is understood that it is the resource owner that is responsible for monopoly.

Notice the vastly different conclusions (specifically how these two approaches regard the role of entrepreneurs and the cause of the origin of monopoly) that result from these different perspectives! These total incompatibilities make it clear that only one approach can be correct.

Traditions tend to be adhered to but not all traditions are valid. Contemporary price theory (Marshallian/neoclassical) treats competition and entrepreneurship in an unsatisfactory manner. Contemporary price theory adopts a fictitious 'economic man' (*Homo oeconomicus*) to facilitate the use of its mathematical models. *Homo oeconomicus* is a simple one-dimensional entity that (not *who*) maximizes material wealth. This one-dimensional entity can be traced directly to the use of an empirical methodology and its equilibrium analysis.

The belief that economic science has to be empirical to be valid is at the heart of this approach. This stems from the time when all the sciences were newly developing in the 1800's and when social scientists had what can be called 'physics envy.' These positivists believed that only by adopting the methods used in the natural sciences, such as physics, could the social sciences develop.

But science has since moved on. No unbiased thinking person sees business firms in the real world as passive price takers, operating in a state of 'perfect competition' where they are locked into a world where nothing changes. It is erroneous to depict 'perfect competition' as a market packed full with no room for anyone else and where each participant is too weak to effect any change in price. Competition means the exact opposite in the real world!

Does contemporary price theory meet the market test? Equilibrium is the tendency but the never-arrived-at-state, so why pretend otherwise? Humans are active and creative rather than passive, automated and mechanical. We want realism in our science so why not analyze the economy as it is, rather than as an imaginary and unrealistic model?

What we know to be true is that human beings act purposefully and that human beings are social creatures; so they cooperate. Which begs the question: What about action? "Action always is essentially the exchange of one state of affairs for another state of affairs."[12, p. 194] It is always our intention to remove uneasiness and to become better off and to improve. However:

> "Strictly speaking, people do not long for tangible goods as such, but for the services which these goods are fitted to render them. They want to attain the increment in well-being which these services are able to convey."[12, p. 233]

The objective, the goal of improvement is the attainment of an 'end.' Generally there are many ways and means available to use to reach those ends and so the natural tendency is to pursue the means of division of labor, which is what enables everyone to contribute in the economy. Isn't this how you function: finding the best way for you to achieve your personal goals?

Economics is the study of the ways and means to attain the ends. Even at this most basic level it is clear and evident that 'purposeful acts' and 'improvements' are not restricted to material goods and services and go beyond mere dollars and cents. There is a qualitative aspect to all human action that is not subject to quantification. Empiricism cannot go there.

This is the reason why the divine microeconomy model, unveiled in Chapter 2, is so significant and powerful, and I must say, timely. And so the truth of the matter is—economics goes beyond the numbers, and even the subjectivist approach to economics continues to advance just like all good science does.

The underlying force of the subjectivist methodology is deductive logic. Deduction moves from theory to facts, from cause to effect, from general law to a particular instance and it is independent of observation.

Subjectivism is the appropriate scientific methodology for the social sciences since you and I make decisions subjectively. For example, the subjective theory of value states that economic goods are "valued subjectively in terms of the satisfaction that the user expects to derive from the incremental use."[10, p. 7]

It is from the exercise of deductive logic that it can be said that: 1) all economic propositions are demonstrably true; 2) that the conclusions are arrived at by working from something that is already known to be true or self-evident; and 3) that they are empirical in the sense that they say something about *real* things.

The best way to prove that an economic theory is about real things is to put it to the market test. We know that the economy is always in disequilibrium tending towards equilibrium. The status quo for disequilibrium is imperfect knowledge and uncertainty. Simply stated, imperfect knowledge and uncertainty are the reasons why the economy always has to be in disequilibrium.

As described by Nobel Laureate F. A. Hayek: information exists "solely as the dispersed bits of incomplete and frequently contradictory knowledge."[3, p. 519] Yet it is our encounters with these bits of knowledge that trigger our responses. Then through a series of systematic changes in the matrix of market decisions the market process manifests itself. A sequence, a process, ensues.

The market process is the appearance of this disequilibrium in an active form. It becomes manifest and evident in the form of a price. Manifestly, "the ultimate source of the determination of prices is the value judgments of the consumers. Prices are the outcome of the valuation preferring *a* to *b*."[12, p. 331] In other words, people give things value.

Why is it so relevant to compare and contrast these two micro-economic theories? To address the relevance of examining the two different approaches to microeconomics I offer the following analogy to emphasize the contrast between contemporary price theory and the competitive entrepreneurship theory. Here is the analogy. The trajectory of a bullet is greatly affected by having the correct bearings at the start. If the bearings are incorrect at the beginning the bullet will miss widely.

We have been considering the realism of these two theoretical approaches, doing so by applying both the market test and logic. If the methodology used is inappropriate the end results will be way off. Real world competition is in no way represented by the 'perfect competition model' which was mentally constructed to just sit and be at rest in the state of equilibrium. In contrast, competitive entrepreneurship is intensely present in the 'real world' state of disequilibrium, as confirmed by the market test. Logic and the market test both make it clear then that the disequilibrium approach is the one that started by using the correct bearings.

The disequilibrium view of the economy, discovered by using the subjectivist methodology, shows that it is the 'market process' where communication and coordination takes place. And it follows logically that acts of intervention impede rather than improve the market process. Notably, those persons who are involved in conducting business and also the entrepreneurs; it is they who are the gems in the market process since they decipher the market information and activate production. Everyone, themselves included, need to know that what they do is extremely beneficial to humankind.

It is my proposition that there is a more insightful definition of, and term for, 'equilibrium' and its irrepressible tendencies. That designation is 'divine economy.' This new designation acknowledges the inherent divine nature of the human being. And it is this divine nature expressed as purposeful action which serves as the building block for the new model.

Consider the logic of a circle. It has no beginning and no end. It is self-contained and whole. Its dimensions are in balance and it is symmetrical. These qualities are symbolically compatible with the concept of equilibrium.

Diagram 1a: New designation for equilibrium

Circles are seen throughout creation, occurring naturally in organic and inorganic forms. Throughout history humans have attributed much significance to all of these qualities of the circle. Now I am using a circle to symbolize the core, the nucleus of the economy. Although the force of equilibrium has no boundaries, unlike the line representing the circumference of the circle, the concept of the centrality of the force of equilibrium in the economy is the dominant feature in the simple model shown in Diagram 1a.

Because of its infinite nature I have chosen to designate the force of equilibrium by a new name. I call it the divine economy.

The economy is a uniquely human institution and the economy works according to its inherently divine nature and its inherent divine power. Implied by this definition, therefore, is that all intervention is artificial and a source of corruption. The equilibrating tendency of the divine economy will eventually destroy any and all of these artificialities.

Before examining in more detail the divine microeconomy model I want to return to the logic of deduction. In my first book in the divine economy theory series, *MORE THAN LAISSEZ-FAIRE*, I introduced the Divine Economy Model©. The Divine Economy Model© is broad and general relative to the model that is newly introduced in this book—the Divine Microeconomy Model©. Following the deductive process I take the Divine Economy Model© and individualize it by going through a series of derivation steps, steps that define the Divine Microeconomy Model©.

In any real sense there is no separation between macro and micro, however, *deducing* by *reducing* takes the model closer to the realm of individual actions, to the realm of our immediate surroundings. And as a consequence new vistas open, as you will see.

❖

Selected Exercises

1. How does contemporary price theory differ from competitive entrepreneurship regarding equilibrium and entrepreneurship? Can they both be correct?

2. In what way does tradition contribute to science and in what way does it stifle science?

Chapter 2
The Essence

Divine Microeconomy Model©

PREFACE

Inside the vessel that was carefully wrapped in the tapestry is a tinted liquid with a slightly viscous nature. It adheres slightly to the vessel walls as it is tilted back and forth. The impression given is that as soon as the stopper is removed a magical fragrance will waft through the air like an aromatic cloud. Excitement builds! No longer able to resist the urge, the stopper is purposefully extracted from the vessel and all of a sudden it is like an olfactory paradise. So palpable is the ecstasy caused by the released essence that the mind seems to register birds warbling their melodies and thunder rumbling in the distance! All things appear as new and organic.

DIVINE MICROECONOMY MODEL ©

This will be a model building experience for you. You may have never had an opportunity before to proceed step by step in an economic model to reach a coherent end. Additionally remarkable, this will be your chance to see first hand how to build a bridge between science and religion. Take your time and enjoy the process.

To begin I need to extract the Divine Economy Model©, Diagram 2f from Chapter 2 in the book entitled *MORE THAN LAISSEZ-FAIRE*. [6, p. 17] In this book that you are now reading, *The HUMAN ESSENCE of Economics*, I will not go into the details about how that divine economy model was formed and developed.

Our starting point will be the same as Diagram 2f entitled "the complete Divine Economy Model independent of time."

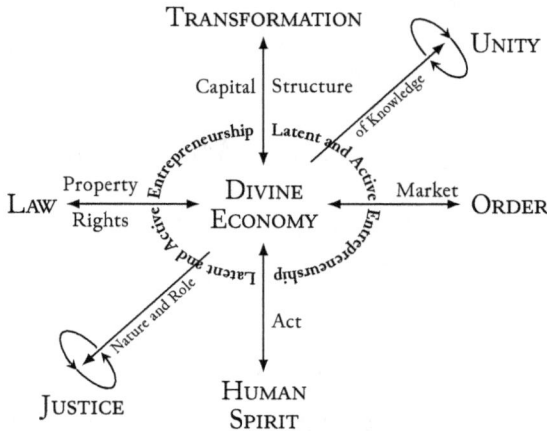

Diagram 2a: The complete Divine Economy Model independent of time

This is quite a complex and dynamic model in all of its applications but what we will take note of here, in particular, is that it is more than a two dimensional model. I now call your attention to the description of the model; notably when the model was transformed from the "Modus Operandi" stage to the "Driving Force of the Divine Economy Model" stage in the process of the unfoldment of the Divine Economy Model©.[6, pp. 15–16] It is clear from the following description that it is more than a two dimensional model: "The next modification of the divine economy model stretches the imagination a little by adding a depth dimension. This can be grasped fairly easily by imagining the modus operandi of the divine economy . . . as submerged in a bowl of water. The water that surrounds and supports the model represents latent and active entrepreneurship."

A more traditionally geometric way to see how the divine economy model takes on a higher dimensional nature comes on pages 16 to 19[6] when there is the addition of the axis called "The Nature and Role of Knowledge." You are probably familiar with three dimensional graphics which show what results from the addition of a *z* axis to a two dimensional graphic with an *x* and a *y* axis.

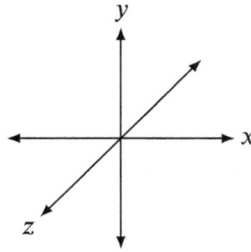

Diagram 2b: A standard three-dimensional figure

In this case we will assume that the "Nature and Role of Knowledge" axis is the z axis and imagine again that the three dimensional model is submerged, immersed in a matrix of latent and active entrepreneurship.

We will now begin assessing the divine economy model from specific vantage points for the purpose of achieving the objective, which is to create the divine microeconomic model. The vantage points will be the end points of each of these principal vectors; x, y and z, looking toward the center of the model. The center of the model represents the equilibrating power which in this model is referred to as the 'divine economy.'

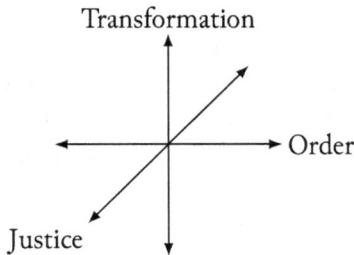

Diagram 2c: x, y, and z vectors of the Divine Economy Model

Looking toward the center from the vantage point of the end of one vector, opens a vista of a two dimensional plane defined by the other two vectors (see Diagram 2d).

This two dimensional plane can be seen not as different from planes that are very familiar to us such as a canvas of a painter, a tablet for verses, or a tapestry of fabric. Now is the best time to mention that all good science comes when science is artfully applied.

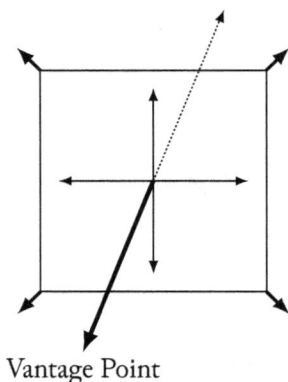

Vantage Point

Diagram 2d: Vantage point view of the two-dimensional plane

The best in their fields of expertise are those who know both the art and the science of their profession and apply it wisely. This tapestry concept for the two dimensional plane is a reminder that there is an art to the application of economic science.

I will now introduce the first stage—the Vantage Point Planes—of the divine microeconomy model. This first stage will show the model as a tapestry from a series of perspectives, as mentioned earlier; perspectives from the ends of each of the six vectors: $-x$, $+x$, $-y$, $+y$, $-z$, and $+z$.

The x axis in the divine microeconomy model is represented by Law $(-x)$ and Order $(+x)$. The plane designation corresponds with the vantage point, so the Law/Order planes are seen in Diagram 2e.

The y axis in the divine microeconomy model is represented by Human Spirit $(-y)$ and Transformation $(+y)$. The Human Spirit/Transformation planes are seen in Diagram 2f.

The z axis in the divine microeconomy model is represented by Justice $(+z)$ and Unity $(-z)$. The Justice/Unity planes are seen in Diagram 2g.

Notice the pattern that I chose for labeling the planes, first one plane then the second one separated by a forward slash (e.g. Law/Order Plane). Although arbitrary to some extent, this naming pattern is motivated strongly by an understanding of cause and effect. Not in an absolute sense do things proceed in this manner but nevertheless there is a very real tendency for this pattern to be the dominant one. For example, if there is justice, unity can be established.

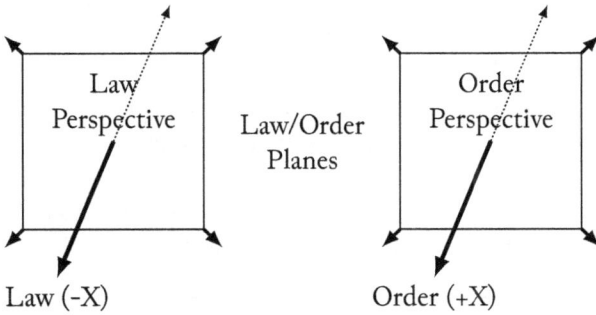

Diagram 2e: View of Law/Order planes

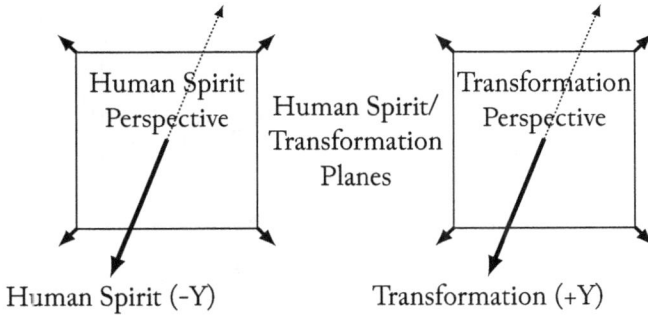

Diagram 2f: View of Human Spirit/Transformation planes

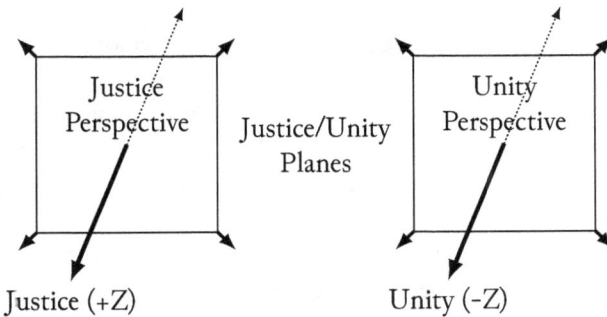

Diagram 2g: View of Justice/Unity planes

What is woven into the fabric of each of these tapestries? What is written upon these tablets? What is painted upon these canvases? The answer: human virtues!

The second stage of the divine microeconomy model, Virtues Akin to the Vantage Point, will be gone into more detail in Chapter 4. Suffice it to say that all these planes are the seats of the human virtues akin to the name of the vantage point. For example, those virtues which reflect the ideal of unity reside on the Unity Plane.

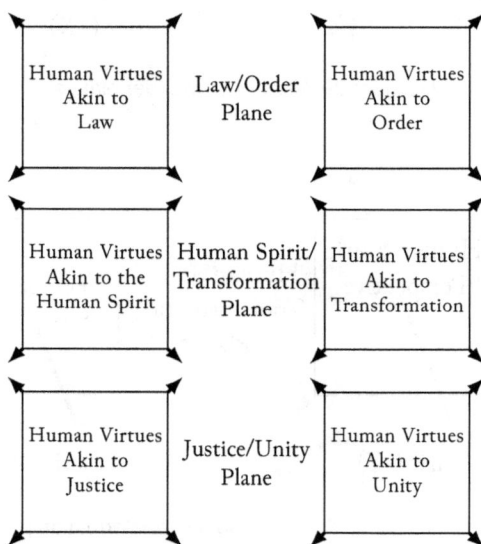

Human Virtues Akin to Law	Law/Order Plane	Human Virtues Akin to Order
Human Virtues Akin to the Human Spirit	Human Spirit/ Transformation Plane	Human Virtues Akin to Transformation
Human Virtues Akin to Justice	Justice/Unity Plane	Human Virtues Akin to Unity

Diagram 2h: Virtues akin to the vantage point

The third and final stage of the divine microeconomy model, which is a divine microeconomic tapestry, incorporates two concepts that are deeply rooted in the human psyche. Our human logic and our understanding of the nature of the origin of things make these two concepts an essential part of human existence. One concept is cause and effect. The other concept is east and west. Both of these concepts appear to be strongly directional; from cause to effect, from east to west. However, the fact that new cycles can and do begin from the end-result shows an important degree of reciprocity.

Stage three introduces cause and effect, and east and west, by adding the element of service to the element of virtue. The symbolism of east and west is compatible with the cause and effect, producing the following pattern: virtue leading to service (or product) which then may stimulate a new cycle. The idea that the acquisition of a virtue (cause) leads to service or a product (effect), which may *inspire* a *desire* to *acquire* more virtue(s) or service, fits the purpose of this model.

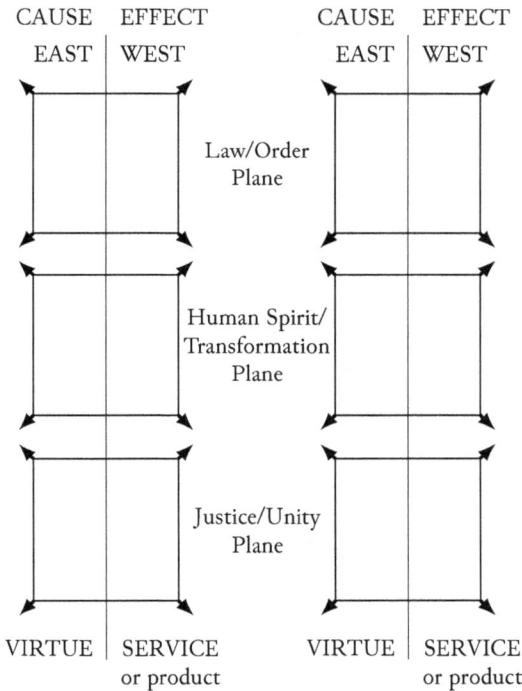

Diagram 2i: Divine Microeconomic Tapestry (also called the Divine Microeconomy Model ©)

Just like the Divine Economy Model ©, this Divine Microeconomy Model © is a complex and dynamic model. Its symmetry and reciprocity carry its essential simplicity forward, making practical applications of the model a real possibility. In essence this is a very powerful economic model!

Selected Exercises

1. Look at Diagram 2a for a moment or two and imagine it as something dynamic and organic. Now align yourself so that you are positioned to look directly along one of the vectors towards the center of the model. Which plane have you chosen to examine?

2. Ponder a moment and then name a virtue that would reside on the plane that you chose. What service to humanity that is valuable in a contractual society emanates from the virtue that you identified to be on the plane that you chose?

Chapter 3
Strands of the Fabric

Core Economic Concepts

Preface

Remembering how silky soft and fine the tapestry wrap felt to the touch we return to examine it more closely. Instantly, and also after thorough examination, the delicate nature and fairness of the silk strands intrigues us. If the strands—the most basic element of the tapestry—are nearly perfect in quality then the potential value of the tapestry must indeed be irrefutably very high. Such is the case with this loving gift.

The Elements

We are about to closely examine how it all works—in the language of economics. The purpose of this chapter is to lay a foundation that cannot be refuted by those who may want to claim that there is no scientific economic rationale behind my model.

I included this rigorous exploration of economic concepts to combat the naysayers. My examination of the core economic concepts is organized in a different manner than usual, and so for this reason, you may find it quite interesting. If you want to stay engaged in reading this book but do not want to go deeper into basic economics, jump directly to Chapter 4 at this point!

As humans we share a pool of knowledge that holds certain concepts and motivations as true. For example, we perceive time as omnipresent and we recognize that our lifetime represents a scarcity of time.

Another way to describe this is to consider our wants. Our desires or wants are unlimited, however time is limited. We find that all of our wants are competitive with each other yet there is a scarcity of means. Nevertheless, whatever it is that we desire, whether it is a material thing or something else, these still remain the object of our quest.

This pursuit—our quest—is selfish (subjective) even if it happens to be a noble deed such as an act of generosity, since we are the ones that know our own selves and we act in our own behalf. Even if we can change our minds about what we consider to be the most valuable 'thing' to us, nevertheless, always what we value is undeniably given a subjective value by us.

In this matrix of people, time, and other resources—the economy—there exists the very great spark of human intelligence. Economic events are causal and complex but the laws that operate in this matrix are simple and universal.

Where do we begin this examination? Everything is so interconnected and interwoven. Wherever we start there will be abundant and continual overlap.

Our goal will be to try to focus and refocus on the individual, to keep ourselves in the microeconomic realm. This is not as easy as it sounds since humans are social beings and prosper in a cooperative society, a contractual society. The prosperity that applies at the level of the individual—like the benefits of voluntary exchange—applies in a comparable manner at the macro level where it would appear as the benefits of trade.

Nevertheless we can and will stay focused. We will accomplish this by adopting the vantage point of the entrepreneur. It is from that point that we will view the microeconomy.

The reason the entrepreneur is the key player in the economy is because of imperfect knowledge. It is the entrepreneur who *seeks information* through the experience of active and alert participation. This is significant since the market process is a discovery process, unfolding through time. The entrepreneurs are the driving force, always moving the economy towards equilibrium.

I dedicate Chapter 6 to entrepreneurs everywhere, by setting it aside to explore their action logic. Now the task at hand is to examine the core microeconomic elements. The core elements are: the individual, demand and supply, prices, production, and profit and loss.

THE INDIVIDUAL

Nothing could be *more* at the *core* than the individual. It is from the very essence of the human reality that both human reason and human action flow since they are 'different aspects of the same thing.'[12, p. 39]

Action is taken at discrete times and places and circumstances rather than in infinitely small intervals along a continuum. Each action rests upon a subjective valuation which is why subjectivism is the appropriate scientific method of analysis.

Individuals progress day by day and moment to moment. This is all a part of the learning process. As a consequence of the learning process there is a pattern of change in an individual's decisions. The unfolding experience of the decisions themselves becomes part of the learning process with the goal being to remove uneasiness and to make oneself better off, that is, to survive and to prosper.

There is a conscious effort aimed at the attainment of the goal. Subjectivism recognizes that the seat of power rests with the individual. Every act of choice or preference entails a sacrifice, an opportunity cost. This subjective valuation is the origin and source of value for all things. Each marginal unit is given a subjective value and each additional unit of a specific good has diminishing utility and therefore diminishing marginal value.

Implied in the action at the margin to achieve one's goal is the use of means. It is the goods or the means capable of satisfying our wants that we value not the wants themselves. These goods and means are used to exchange one state of affairs for another.

This can happen by barter but the truth of the matter is that we are in a relatively modern era of economics for the simple reason that a more efficient method of the means of exchange—money—predominates.

Once money was developed to facilitate indirect exchange, prices emerged. But don't be fooled by prices. Know what they represent. Subjective values are ordinal not cardinal so the exchange price is sufficient for the exchange to occur, but it is not an objective valuation. Exchange takes place because there is a double inequality of wants between the trading partners. Each market participant values what they get more than what they give up. This interconnectedness with others brings about relative prosperity resulting from maximizing exchange transactions for mutual benefit.

Exchanges also represent valuable learning experiences. This learning process is more formally described as the market process, which is the 'place' where people embark on a knowledge gaining series, *each one more competitive than the preceding period*. It is impossible to have an economy without the market process.

In this marketplace world there is division of labor; individuals acting as resource owners and entrepreneurs and capitalists and laborers. Individuals exercise their property rights, they voluntarily exchange, and by taking human action they convey to the rest of the world their sovereignty as consumers — to be served by the market.

So despite the fact that there are latent elements in the economy and that sometimes resource owners and consumers are price-takers, the market operates — thanks to those who are the alert to opportunities. The consequence of this competitive entrepreneurship is the connecting of the desires of the consumers with everything needed to satisfy those desires. Take a moment to think deeply about the following statement: resource prices or 'costs' are derived from the expected prices of the consumers' goods that the resources were used to produce. In other words, all values throughout the market are attributed to the values ultimately given by consumers.

One thing we know for sure is that everyone prefers to have lower prices and better quality. Not coincidentally this is the direction of the forces of competitive entrepreneurship. Immediately it becomes clear that competitive entrepreneurship serves everyone by bringing about lower prices and higher quality.

Competition and entrepreneurship are analytically inseparable in the market. The entrepreneurial alertness to these hitherto unnoticed opportunities is almost always exercised throughout the economy by many individuals at the same time. It is not the entrepreneurs who are generating the opportunities *per se*, but rather, alertly responding to opportunities is their function in the market.

The individual, referred to in the economic literature as '*Homo agens*' is endowed with the propensity for alertness. Alertness is why the market is universally a learning experience and why fresh goals are continually surfacing and why previously unknown resources are discovered.

And finally let it be known that individuals are at the beginning of it all, their subjective value is at the origin, and it is their decisions about what to consume that is ultimately the sovereign mandate. Business firms do provide a vital function but ultimately it is the individuals who need to protect economic freedom. That is their right and their responsibility.

DEMAND AND SUPPLY

Proceeding now into another aspect of economic science we will examine the law of demand. The demand curve is 'falling' because it is rooted in marginal utility. As you and I—consumers—see it: as the number of units of a particular good increases each one satisfies a lower degree of want so the chance that the marginal utility of a good exceeds the price of a good is greater as the price lowers. As prices go down the quantity demanded goes up. Translation: people prefer lower prices!

Demand is not the same as wants. Wants are unlimited whereas demand is a function of purchasing power. Therefore demand ultimately comes from productive effort and the income derived from that effort. Demand for a good indicates the preference for acquiring a good or service at the various prices. The demand then is a representation of the response to price. The lower the price the more will be purchased. It is the quantity demanded that changes as prices change.

Supply, on the other hand, is what is necessary to overcome scarcity. Since the wants are unlimited but the means are limited it is production that ameliorates this condition. In other words, production is the source of supply. Changes in demand and supply manifest themselves in the market as the dynamic and ever-present disequilibrium.

At any specific point in time production has already occurred and there is a certain market price where exchanges are taking place which means that, right then and there, the supply curve is vertical. The 'snapshot' taken at that specific point in time is not realistic in terms of it being economically comprehensive, but it will nevertheless prove to be instructive. See Diagram 3a.

Ultimately it will be market demand that determines prices but consumers' preferences are dynamic, ever-changing. As a result, market demand is always veiled in uncertainty but the best way to find out more information is to enter into the marketplace. Producers do just that and they enter with a price in mind (not knowing the true market price), an

Price

Diagram 3a: Snapshot of the demand, supply, and market price

estimated price that indicates to the producer that a profit opportunity exists. Thus a production plan is set forth in terms of the expected price per unit and the estimated number of units to produce.

Once the production program is completed the finished product will enter the market. Here is the snapshot of the market as faced by the producers for that particular planned sales period:

Diagram 3b: What is the market telling you to do?

The market clearing price is the price at which all of the product would be sold by the end of the 'planned sales period.'[9, p. 191] The minimum reserve price assumes that the product is non-perishable and could be put in storage for future sale if prices in the market are too low right now. In other words, no producer is willing to sell any units of the product below that minimum reservation price during this sales period.

Firms selling their product at the market clearing price of $3.25 will be able to sell all of their products within that sales period. Now looking at Diagram 3b we can see what happens if the producer estimates the market demand incorrectly. Firm A expected to be able to get $4.25 per unit but at that price not all units will be sold. There will be 'x minus A' number of units unsold ($Q_s > Q_d$).

The firm(s) selling at $2.25 per unit will sell out before the end of the selling period ($Q_s < Q_d$). The shortage is represented by 'B minus x' with x being the units sold but B being the units needed to be sold in that sales period at that price.

If firms experience surpluses or shortages it is because they chose a disequilibrium price in their ex ante estimate. Ex post the market demand ultimately confirms or refutes the ex ante estimates of price and quantity. Adjustments need to be made and they are made.

Trying to portray a more realistic picture necessitates consideration of market disequilibrium and all of the systematic alterations in the pattern of prices and quantities, and also the systematic alterations in the pattern of product types and qualities, in an environment of competitive pressure. For instance, "a variety of product qualities may be produced for no other reason than that equilibrium has not been reached."[5, p. 115] Crucial to understanding this series of systematic changes in the interconnected network of market decisions is recognizing how the competitive nature created by entrepreneurial alertness brings about changes in the buying, selling, producing and consuming decisions that make up the market process.

All of this dynamic action cannot be fully captured by a line graph. So what then is the relevance of the demand and supply curves to the

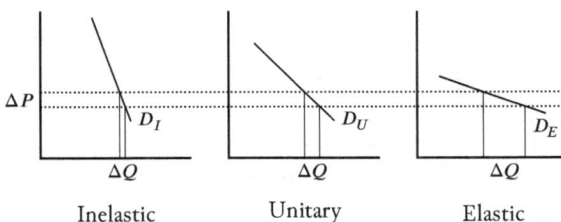

Diagram 3c: Demand elasticities

real world? The demand curve is a representation of the response to price. The more responsive to price, the more elastic the demand is said to be.

If the demand is inelastic there will not be much of a change in the quantity demanded if the price changes. If there is unitary elasticity the change in the quantity demanded will be proportional to the change in the price. If the demand is elastic the quantity demanded changes quite dramatically if the price changes.

The more choices there are in the minds of the consumer the more elastic the demand is to price. Necessarily the price elasticity faced by a firm is greater than for an industry. This is true because there are other competing firms to buy from, in other words, there are more choices.

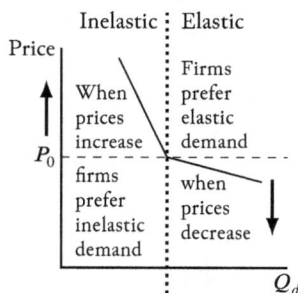

Diagram 3d: The ideal price elasticity from the perspective of the firm

Price elasticity reflects the complex interaction of close substitutes, competition, size of its relative price (e.g., consider the impact of a price cut on a high-priced item), the relative importance of the item (ones with strict minimum requirements), and the existing stock on hand; but it is consumers and not the firms that ultimately determine elasticity.

A businessperson, by the trial and error of changing prices (Table 3a), can get a sense for the degree of price elasticity within a certain price range associated with a particular product at a specific point in time. This very specific information—revealed as a total revenue schedule for that segment of the demand schedule—may have value in some cases.

The total revenue equals price times quantity ($TR = P \times Q$). Sometimes total revenue may not remain the same when the price changes. If a firm lowers (or raises) its prices the total revenue may increase, decrease or remain the same. Refer to this equation, $TR = P \times Q$, when reading the next sentence. If P (price) decreases (causing quantity demanded to increase) yet total revenue decreases then there is relative inelasticity. The following table shows these relationships.

Price Change	Change in Q_d	Change in total revenue as an indicator of the degree of elasticity of demand	
$P \downarrow$	$Q_d \uparrow$	$+TR$	If Elastic
		$-TR$	If Inelastic
		No Change	If Unitary
$P \uparrow$	$Q_d \downarrow$	$-TR$	If Elastic
		$+TR$	If Inelastic
		No Change	If Unitary

Table 3a: How is total revenue affected by demand elasticities?

Here is another point of relevance: since firms face a more elastic demand curve than does an industry the equilibrium forces inherent in the market economy would tend to break any attempt to form a cartel. This is because: if a firm charges a lower price than the cartel price the result would be a significant change in the quantity demanded from the firm (drawing buyers industry-wide) and total revenue would increase for the firm. The increased total revenue is an irresistible incentive, enticing a firm to break the cartel.

PRICES

People value things. The things they value, and also the resources (factors) that are needed to produce those things, are valuable because they are scarce. Prices and scarcity are interrelated and interdependent but ultimately prices are determined by market demand.

Each thing is assessed independently, based on its marginal utility. The value of each thing is subjectively ascribed to it by individuals and is reflected in their purchasing decisions. Relative prices emerge as a result of this process in the market and they are the most widespread aspect of the market.

What does this process represent? "The market prices tell the producers what to produce, how to produce, and in what quantity."[12, p. 258] It is the fact that people value things determinedly that leads to a fulfillment of their valuations.

Fulfillment of this valuation process is a description of what the market does. It is impossible to have an economy without markets. The market process is where the real world risks and uncertainties characteristic of the state of disequilibrium are overcome by the mechanism of prices and profit and loss, leading to the satisfaction of people's needs and desires, even to the extent of capturing the non-price influences.

What is price? If I see the price go down for one of the goods that I desire, to me that is a good thing. A variant to this but still a 'price' is: if I see the quality of a good go up yet I still only pay the same price as earlier, that is a good thing. Both of these 'prices' are driven by equilibrium forces; the result of the forces of supply and demand. Decisions to buy and sell are pegged to this pivot, the price, the carrier of information.

Competitive pressures that occur in the dynamic state of market disequilibrium cause adjustments to be made in the pattern of prices and quantities but also in the pattern of product types and qualities. These pattern pressures influencing both price and quality are inseparable and analogous. The influence of the market forces affects prices, quantities and product qualities, styles, sizes, color, packaging and so on.

Prices also convey information to the seller. Their product is offered on the market at a speculative price but if the price is not ideal (equilibrium) the market feedback mechanism will send signals of disequilibrium. Unless the seller's chosen price happens to be the market clearing price (equilibrium) potentially there will either be a shortage or a surplus of that good for that planned sales period. Price adjustments will need to be made.

In the real world, entrepreneurs and businesspeople are concerned with 'prices' because they affect total revenue ($TR = P \times Q$). In the real world, successful market clearing (optimal total revenue) is due mostly to good fortune. What are the chances that the entrepreneurial plans of the producer coincide exactly with the objective market conditions? Most of the time price adjustments will need to be made.

Resource prices (or costs) are proportional to the expected end value of the consumer good that comes at the end of the production cycle. "The prices of the goods of higher orders are ultimately determined by the prices of the goods of the first or lower order, that is, the consumers' goods."[12, p. 333] If the consumer doesn't value some thing enough it will not be produced, neither will factors be used for that purpose. There are prices throughout the system and they all convey vital information.

Prices coordinate the system throughout all stages of production and at the end stage of consumption. From the end point the consumer demand infuses prices backward throughout the system. Ultimately, it is the consumers that determine prices and also the price elasticities of all goods and services.

It is towards consumer sovereignty, meeting their needs and wants, that producers must orient themselves. The firm enters the market with a price in mind but not knowing the true market price. Accordingly this producer has already committed to producing x units in this particular production cycle. This is the beginning of the drama that unfolds. In this opening act adjustments will need to be made. As the drama unfolds we encounter the unpredictable features of the market: uncertainty and changes taking place over time. It is an unending drama, richly human.

In a free market the equilibrium tendency drives the expected price of a good in the future (minus the pure interest) towards equalization with the price of a good in the present. There is also a tendency toward the establishment of a uniform price for the same good throughout the world which includes wage rates for the same degree of ability. These tendencies necessarily exist due to arbitrage which comes from awareness of price discrepancies and then action to capture the margins.

The ratio of the proportional difference between the expected price of a good in the future and the price of that good in the present, apart from uncertainty and risk, is also a price—pure interest—and it is an estimate of the time preference of that culture. It is this price ratio expressed as a percent that is a representation of time preference. The greater the time preference the greater is the pure interest rate. Time preference limits the investment of time, labor and land and therefore it limits the amount and structure of capital.

To continue to understand how prices coordinate the system through-out all the stages of production consider the difference between a good now and the same good a year from now. The price of the good one year from now equals the present price + costs of storage + allowance for the going rate of profit on the capital (based on the cultural time preference) that must be invested in storage.

Prices are infused throughout the economy and across the time horizon. As a result of competition and entrepreneurial action prices are imputed to each factor according to its marginal value product, which means—according to its productive share of the whole. Price formation in the market economy is the means of measuring the goodness of a good.

PRODUCTION

Producers serve either directly or indirectly. Production has value attributed to it subjectively by consumers because it ameliorates the condition of scarcity. Scarcity exists because humans have limited means but unlimited wants. Ultimately the purpose of production is consumption.

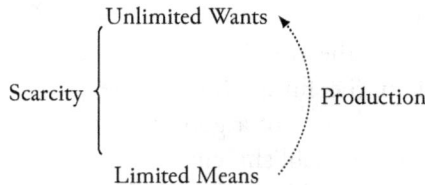

Diagram 3e: Scarcity and what alleviates it

Economics is the study of the means to attain the ends; so needless to say, production is a major economic topic. For goals to be met scarce resources are needed. Production is the conversion of resources into specialized goods and services through the division of labor. Goods produced either satisfy wants directly (meaning the actual consump-tion of the good) or indirectly by facilitating the production process, ultimately towards consumption.

The impetus behind production is the consumer's desire for better quality, more choices and lower prices. Of course, production is prior to consumption. Consumers have the power to change the course of production by changing their spending patterns. Prices for factors come backwards from consumption and all of these market prices tell the producers what to produce and in what quantity. Being alert in this competitive environment, it is the producer who serves as a 'built-in' entrepreneur.

Production that leads to more choices, to better quality and/or lower prices raises the standard of living. Production will be either for direct use or a part of the market division of labor. Production that yields an increase in capital goods leads to a higher standard of living in the future.

One omnipresent limitation is time! Production takes time. And since production is a time consuming process it aligns itself with the time preferences of the consumers. Time preference for present goods manifests itself as a restraint on future goods, that is, on any and all such investment of time, labor, land and capital. Prices throughout the economy serve to convey this differential information.

The producer, acting like an entrepreneur in a competitive environment, searches high and low for profit opportunities. The producer (*as if it is easy*) merely needs to know where to buy resources at a price worthwhile to produce, such that the product can be sold at an attainable price in the future! Once found the producers' actions signal that a discovery was made.

The first stage of production just after this 'discovery' is ex ante; estimating, speculating, planning and investing. The second stage follows, which is the act of physical production signaling that a previously unperceived revenue possibility may indeed have been found. This is the 'announcement' made by beginning production.

As part of the production process there is what is called a derived demand for factors of production. Resource owners who find the payment offered by producers sufficiently attractive to make them willing to sell their resources do so. Wage earners fit into this category. Resource owners can also play the role of a capitalist if they are willing to sell their resources under an agreement which promises them revenue only at some time in the future.

Once labor is added to other resources it becomes either a capital good or a final consumption good. What is a capital good, or another variation on that question, what is capital? "Capital is a way station along the road to the enjoyment of consumers' goods."[8, p. 52] Seeing capital as 'works in progress' demonstrates that capital has time structure.

Production requires investment. Capital is savings and investment that pays resource owners now even though there is no revenue yet. However, capital is not an independent productive factor since it depends on land, labor and time for any and all capital to accumulate. Again, saving and investing are necessary to build anything.

The time market, where the interest rate is the all-important price, permeates the entire production structure. Since there is alertness to all price discrepancies, the interest rate will tend to be uniform within and across the various stages of production (when there is no intervention). There are competitive pressures that cause this tendency; and these competitive pressures come from the purchasing of producers' goods and services of any and all kinds at any point throughout the production structure of the economy. It turns out that this type of credit—taking advantage of the capital made available by these resource owners—is an even more important use of the 'time market' than the loan market.

Practically speaking there are two types of productive endeavors in the economy. Either long processes that are more productive or short processes that are less productive. These have to be chosen from and it is a relative abundance of savings and investment which makes it possible to choose the processes that take a long time.

There are three types of production for use-value. The first one is production for a more useful *form*. The second is production for the *place* more preferred or more valued. And finally there is production that is made available at a more desirable *time*. Capital and especially the combination of capital and storage make time production feasible. Producers' goods are examples of time use-value.

Due to the equilibrating power of arbitrage the economy operates and is characterized by the tendency towards the principle of uniformity-of-profit. This is what keeps in proper balance the production of all types, and of all of the different items that are directly or indirectly necessary for our survival.

If in any one period the competitive process comes to a halt it does not mean a failure of the process. Disequilibrium—the real world condition—is characterized by widespread ignorance, meaning that despite all the alertness that market participants have they still are unaware of all of the opportunities that exist. In this sense the competitive process is in a 'potential' state but as soon as the opportunities are perceived they will be pursued in a most competitive way.

From beginning to end what does production look like? "The production process of a typical 'commodity' consists of raw materials which must be gathered and worked on. Machinery and other factors used in production must be obtained, set up, repaired, etc. When the final product emerges it must be insured, transported and kept track of. It must be advertised and retailed. Records must be kept, legal works must be done, and the finances must be in good order."[2, p. 166]

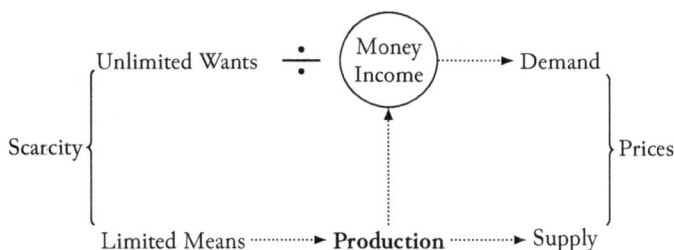

Diagram 3f: Production as the progenitor

The producer estimates the selling price and the numbers of units to produce for the first planned sales period. As the results in the market become known adjustments are made to minimize disappointment before the end of the planned sales period. At the same time a new strategy is formulated for the next time around, fully aware that the market is always changing.

Some empiricists try to dissect production for the purpose of examining 'efficiency' but we already covered how it is the equilibrating tendencies and forces in the economy that make it inherently efficient. Examples of these forces at work are arbitrage and competitive entrepreneurship.

There is a seamless nature to production. Everyone along the way contributes, everyone along the way is a 'middleman.' The process of production includes every step, all the way up until the good is consumed, including making the consumer aware of the availability of the product and the desirability of the product. Everywhere along the production line someone playing this particular role of a middleman will perform this service. All of these 'selling costs' are all a part of the process.

Since consumers are often passive entrepreneurs it is the producer who must complete the production process by taking active steps to get the potential customers to know about these purchase opportunities. Producers reduce the uncertainty of the total supply on the market by product differentiation but this then suggests that the producer needs to educate the consumers about the product.

If the price signals have not been tampered with and if the producers correctly assessed the situation, then all the costs of production will have been initially anticipated. Production began because the producer anticipated that the consumer would value the product more than the sum total of all of the costs of production. To complete our understanding of Diagram 3f we need to remember that only production is the source of income and only production is the source of the supply of goods and services that can reduce or modify scarcity.

In the real world of uncertainty and imperfect knowledge there are no guarantees. The market process ultimately determines the selling price and the market price determines all costs. (Remember the backward reaching effect of derived demand?) In the end the result may be a profit or it may be a loss. And since production can continue only if it yields positive results (i.e., yielding a profit) there are limits to production. Unequivocally, it must be clearly stated that there is nothing evil about profit. It is what motivates production despite the uncertainty!

PROFIT AND LOSS

This is the climax, the culmination. Individual action—captured in demand and supplied by production at the price that brings into harmony demand and supply—is for the sake of generating income so the good(s) desired can be purchased. Profit, directly or indirectly, is the prime generator of incomes.

It is inaccurate to describe human beings as merely profit maximizing economizers! First of all, decisions made by humans are not simply monetary. There is a psychic cost, the lost 'utility' of the next best alternative that one has to forgo, to every action taken. And there is a psychic revenue that results from the increase in happiness that comes from the action chosen.

In this sense profit is purely subjective and cannot be measured. Even if we were speaking about both monetary and non-monetary profit, profit maximization is a fleeting thing since the real world is always in a state of disequilibrium, never really reaching equilibrium.

Prices that are stated in the terms of the medium of exchange do facilitate the recognition of what is valued. Once the economy evolved to the point of adopting a medium of exchange all things were expressed in those terms. This major advancement of the economy took us out of the barter economy and made it possible for another innovation —accounting—and opened the door to a better understanding of profit and loss.

We humans, endowed with the propensity for alertness and classified as *Homo agens*, act upon the information about what is valuable. Some are passive, only finding ways to increase their own happiness. Others are out there as profit seekers, and their actions benefit everyone.

These profit seekers try to identify the relevant ends–means framework and how to make it more efficient. Through their efforts to discover price differentials throughout the economy and along the time horizon they bring to the surface market knowledge. Their actions benefit themselves but also everyone else.

What we have are price searchers; not the imaginary price-takers conjured up by the empirical economists. What is sought are the price terms and other contractual terms that work best given the constraints of the preferences of the consumers and given the competitive offers being made by alternative suppliers.

It is in this competitive and entrepreneurial condition where the profit seeker perceives something special, like when a good can be sold at a price higher than that for which it or the sum of its precursors can be bought, given the time preferences of the consumers. If that perception turns out to be true there will be a profit. If not, a loss.

The fact that some will make a profit, that some will just break even, and that some will take a loss is not problematic. First of all, the scale of the endeavors is widely various so that no one has to be tested beyond their abilities. Second, there is freedom to either be actively or passively alert to what is going on in the market. And third, the continual and dynamic process of the selection of the fittest makes sure that it is primarily the most efficient entrepreneurs who are offering their services for the benefit of all.

Profit seeking is just that—seeking. There is no guarantee. The profit seeker is a risk taker that uses market prices to determine what to produce or what can be produced more efficiently. The risks taken to initiate new production or improved production will yield various outcomes such as: lower price, better quality, and/or product differentiation.

The enticing wonder of the discovery of a profit opportunity, which keeps the entrepreneur coming back and entering into the market process, is the discovery of something obtainable for nothing at all. It is the same as the quest of the explorer and the artist and the scientist and the philosopher—to discover something never known before. The profit seeking motive is this same motivation, this same human phenomenon. Therefore as you can see, the profit seeking motive is part of the human operating system, something to be appreciated—not to be condemned as an evil.

The 'nuts and bolts' of profit and loss is $TR - TC$ (total revenue minus total costs). If changing the price increases the total revenue, then because of the profit motive, that is what will be done. If changing the product quality improves profitability then that is what will be done. If making production more efficient (lowering total costs) makes the endeavor more profitable that is what will begin to happen.

These types of exploration for improved profitability constantly and perpetually motivate the profit seekers. If someone decides to stop their exploration, then someone else will make the discoveries and will capture the profits.

In the real world it is the producer who most often takes on the role of perceiving and making changes, motivated by profit opportunities. Many of the opportunities for more efficient use of resources simply go unnoticed by non-producers because only those who are involved in the production process actually encounter them or understand them. Often these opportunities are the result of imperfect coordination between transactions in the resource markets and in the product markets. By involvement in the market process profit seekers create the possibility of greater cooperation between otherwise disconnected segments of the economy.

Profit seeking has a revelatory effect in the economy. Seeking profit opportunities by examining them relative to each other, reveals what people want. This continually directs resources towards the production of those particular goods and services. The reason differential profits are possible in the real world is because not all firms are equally innovative or even able to mimic the innovation of others. In the real world innovation is an advantage, yielding differential profits because there is a lag time before others can catch up. The talents and creativity within firms is not equal and so part of the competitors' strategy to catch up with the innovator is to lure away key personnel, along with intensifying both market research and product research and development.

As a consequence, profit seeking advances the tendency towards homogeneity, ironically offsetting the tendency for product differentiation. Necessarily, the tendency is for the rate of profit among close competitors to become equalized. Economy-wide profit-seeking leads to the tendency for profits in all of the different fields of endeavor to equalize in the market.

All investors face the reality that the return on their investment is uncertain. Will the skilled worker get a return on the investment made to acquire those skills? Will the capitalist get a return on the savings invested?

Despite the constant changes in prospective earnings and related changes in capital values there are those who can successfully discount future prices. A premium is placed on the individual or the firm that is able to successfully read the uncertain future. Working back from a profitable expected selling price in a way that incorporates the sought-after profit margin and that determines the limit to factor outlays (per unit) is no easy task. Investors are looking for the firms that can do this successfully.

Market demand is out there. The profitable firms hold onto consumers' demand by the means of product differentiation, and they innovate, lowering costs and prices. All of this catches the attention of investors. Since investors prefer profitable firms more capital is made available to them. Alert firms that command sufficient capital funds will be the ones that fill the market demand gaps.

Any decisions by the profit seeker to proceed, to go forward with production plans, is a declaration that there is an opportunity to convert the upcoming expenditures into a profit, once the future revenue stream begins to flow. These alterations, newly added to the market, set in motion systematic changes in the interconnected network of market decisions. The new knowledge infused into the market process alters the conditions of uncertainty and imperfect knowledge as it necessarily cascades throughout.

Armed with the knowledge that the expected benefit in the forecasted future warrants incurring today's costs, the endeavor begins. The significant test will be the market price itself which serves as the testing ground for sales and profit expectations. Facing the actual state of demand—the market price—the producer is then in the ex post and making adjustments most successfully depends on having some knowledge of the elasticity of demand.

In the ex post it is time to be alert to the sales status for the planned sales period. If sales are as expected then the market price is the same as the estimated market clearing price and profits will be optimal. If instead there appears to be disequilibrium outcomes—a shortage or a surplus—then the ability to adjust to the market conditions will determine the income fate of all participants in the production process.

But already the producer needs to prepare for the next planned sales period, the next time around (NTA).[9, p. 199] Based on the ex post results of the prior planned sales period, if a surplus is projected at the 'current price A' there are three choices, all designed to *maximize profits by minimizing losses*. The producer could lower the selling price but what this means is that to be able to maintain the present profit

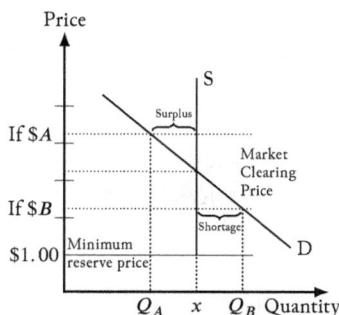

Diagram 3g: Maximizing profits by minimizing losses

margin costs must be cut. This could mean job losses. Or the producer could reduce the supply by cutting production. This could also mean the loss of jobs. Another option would be to try a combination of these, with the goal being to maximize profits by minimizing losses.

To adjust to a projected shortage for the next time around the producer could raise the price and face the social taboo associated with raising prices or he or she could increase the supply via an influx of capital investment thereby improving the production process and lowering marginal costs. Of course there are risks due to the uncertainty of the market demand. Enlarging productive capacity to increase the supply and to lower the unit costs may not prove to be necessary in the long run.

Why take the risk? The margin between the selling price and the per unit cost of a product, the price spread, is enticing as long as it is equal to or greater than other opportunities, such as earnings from investing in financial assets instead of production. Since production is the most basic of all endeavors it is always a prime candidate for investment. Potentially, profits emerge from production.

Profit has three components. The pure interest component is shared alike by production for profit and by other investments earning interest. What is expected for sacrificing present consumption for future consumption is the pure interest component. It is an expression of the natural time preference. No action would be taken if this pure interest component is not present.

The second component is entrepreneurial profit which comes about because the future is unknown. Ex ante estimates for production and price are educated guesses, with a certain amount of entrepreneurial profit potential. Astute entrepreneurial perception may lead to a lessening of the risks taken despite the uncertainty faced. Alertness then to the market reaction—ex post—is mostly where the entrepreneurial profit component is captured. For instance if excess demand is discovered early in the selling period a raising of the price would lead to increased profits making the entrepreneurial component of the profits larger. Of course also, a lack of entrepreneurial perception could lead to losses.

The third profit component is the purchasing power spread. This element is mostly seen nowadays as a phenomenon of monetary intervention which causes the purchasing power of the currency to decrease due to inflating the money supply. A profit margin has to be built into the ex ante price because it takes time before the product reaches the market. Ex post the purchasing power will have declined when there is inflation making real profits significantly less than nominal profits.

The 'loss' half of 'profit and loss' occurs when there is a negative return on the investment. In general, the greater the potential of gain (or loss) faced by the investors the greater the risk. Losses in a market economy are just as necessary as profits since they also serve to allocate limited resources. This is what happens efficiently in an unhampered market economy.

Since profit is the prime generator of other incomes the destructive effect of monetary economic intervention on interest rates and on both entrepreneurial profit and the purchasing power component of profit have repercussions and reverberations throughout the economy. Other types of economic intervention (e.g., regulations) also constrain prices or production causing either shortages or surpluses that cannot be remedied by the natural market processes because of the coercive characteristics of the intervention. This is what happens in the unnatural condition of a hampered economy because it is being subjected to this type of political corruption of the economy.

Back to the unhampered economy, notice that most of the time the ex ante expectations need modified during the planned sales period. In other words, producer/entrepreneurs are trying to maximize profits mostly by minimizing losses. This is a little different from the ideal, the real objective, which is to reach the point of optimal profit which occurs when $MR = MC$.

Market information is very elusive because demand is fickle since it is a function of the subjective valuations of consumers, which can and do change over time. Of course this makes market information difficult to ascertain. Only engagement within the market process reveals this information for each selling period. Profit maximization is more a result of minimizing losses by entrepreneurial actions than actually attaining the point on the graph!

Those who are removed from the market and who are out of touch with how production needs to change to meet the demand cannot contribute anything. These are the empirical economists! They assume away the essential characteristics of how demand really operates in

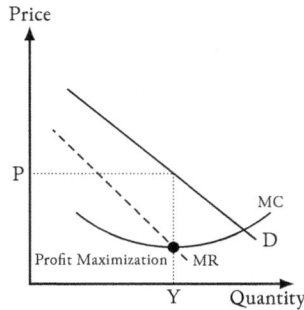

Diagram 3h: Demand and marginal revenue and profit maximization

the market—that it is intimately tied to subjective valuation. That erroneous fantasy is the starting point of their arbitrary and destructive economic intervention.

In the unhampered free market we have individuals, demand and supply, prices, production, and profit and loss all working beautifully to allocate limited resources to meet the unlimited wants as best as possible. Ultimately then, it is the profit motive of the profit seeker that acts upon the market process, stimulating production to increasingly meet the needs of the consumer. Therefore it can be said that the profit motive serves as an agent of continuous economic progress.

❖

Selected Exercises

1. Regarding the individual, *Homo sapiens* indicates that humans are wise and *Homo agens* indicates that humans are agents of alertness. Describe how competitive entrepreneurship fits the economic behavior of individuals.

2. Regarding demand and supply, describe the disequilibrium in the market and how supply initiates knowledge of the state of affairs in the market.

3. Regarding prices, use language as an analogy to describe how prices work throughout the market and across the time horizon.

4. Regarding production, what would happen to production if speculation is restricted in any way because of ill-informed economic intervention?

5. Regarding profit and loss, how human would we be if the artist or the explorer or the scientist was deprived of the act of discovery? Describe why the discovery of a profit opportunity is a beautifully human act which benefits everyone.

Chapter 4
Weft And Warp

The Harmony of
Economic Science and Religion

PREFACE

Why was the gift wrapped in an exquisite silk? For practical reasons the vessel carrying the essence needed to be protected and this was accomplished very well by the tightly woven silk strands of this fabric. The interlocking fibers added much beauty and the binding together of the weft and warp added strength, elasticity and durability, guaranteeing its integration with the vessel and adding to the integrity and the value of the gift.

Tightly woven together at the microeconomic level are thoughts and ideas, and the threads of human action. The fabric of the realities — the virtues — makes the divine microeconomy tapestry a source of prosperity for everyone.

EPISTEMOLOGICAL PURSUIT

It is not my intention to delve deeper into microeconomics — and to go to soul-stirring depths — simply because it may be fashionable, neither is it because it may be unfashionable. I am a scientist seeking high and low, seeking everywhere, along the path of truth — wherever it leads.

Science loses its power and purpose if it cannot go beyond the familiar. I disagree with the direction of some contemporary thought: "It is no longer fashionable in political science to refer to 'self-evident principles.' Indeed, any reference to self-evident or axiomatic propositions is taken to be evidence that a scholar is leaving the realm of science and entering a mysterious netherworld consisting of tautologies, definitions, and metaphysical statements."[1]

According to the above statement, limits are placed on science. However, the scope of human science encompasses more than observation. It has a philosophical basis. The branch of philosophy which investigates the origin, nature, methods and limits of human knowing is called epistemology. Epistemology is worthy of any attention given to it in the past, in the present, or in the future.

DUALISM

Dualism is part of the nature of the human being. There is the body and there is the mind. What about the dualism implied with regard both good and evil? How can opposites be a part of the same thing? It is the concept of dualism that allows humans to be described as both physical and spiritual.

Whatever direction a person is going, they are alive, having sentience and therefore they are an embodiment of change. Human beings are dynamic not static. In terms of moving in a direction, individuals progress day by day, moment by moment.

What about an assessment of progress? Necessarily there is dualism in the assessment also. To the human being, which has more value: a sumptuous dinner alone or a simple sandwich and soup with dear friends? If I value the love of my spouse it must be true that I consider it real, mustn't it?

Because human beings know things that are physical and know things that are spiritual both are seen as realities. Interestingly, as the lower aspirations—which tend to be physical needs—are fulfilled, higher aspirations are sought. The higher aspirations like love, loyalty, and friendship are not physical things; nevertheless they are the realities, the realities of human beings who are in a state of higher aspirations.

Methodological dualism defines the seemingly insurmountable bridge between "the external world of physical, chemical and physiological phenomena and the internal world of thought, feeling, valuation and purposeful action."[12, p. 18] The cusp of social sciences is always near this enigma. The exploration of the human mind is the task at hand and it will be a task of primary importance for the foreseeable future.

Consider one evident manifestation of dualism: the act of rational self-interest that ultimately leads to the well-being of all. This is the very essence of the divine economy! As you can see the divine economy must be profound indeed!

THE VIRTUES PLANES

To begin the work of bridging the gap between science and religion at the microeconomic level I chose the 52 universally recognized virtues identified in *The Family Virtues Guide*[4]. My placement of these fifty-two virtues into the various Vantage Point Planes is arbitrary and is itself potentially a learning exercise for anyone who makes such an attempt. The outcome is quite revealing as you will soon see in Diagram 4b.

Meanwhile, Diagram 4a reveals that there is symmetry and reciprocity that extends across the aperture that exists between science and religion.

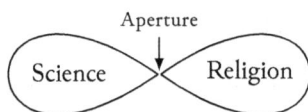

Aperture

Science   Religion

Diagram 4a: Trying to grasp infinity (∞)!

Identifying the human characteristics behind the actions, as part of the attempt to better understand economics, is not without precedent. In *Human Action* Ludwig von Mises writes the following:

> "The buyer must always rely upon the trustworthiness of the seller. Even in the purchase of producers' goods the buyer, although as a rule an expert in the field, depends to some extent on the reliability of the seller. This is still more the case on the market for consumers' goods. Here the seller for the most part excels the buyer in technological and commercial insight. The salesman's task is not simply to sell what the customer is asking for. He must often advise the customer how to choose the merchandise which can best satisfy his needs. The retailer is not only a vendor; he is also a friendly helper. The public does not heedlessly patronize every shop. If possible, a man prefers a store or a brand with which he himself or trustworthy friends have had good experience in the past.

Law/Order Plane	
Cleanliness Courtesy Faithfulness Honesty Love Modesty Obedience Reverence Steadfastness	Consideration Detachment Flexibility Idealism Moderation Orderliness Peacefulness Responsibility Trust
Human Spirit/ Transformation Plane	
Confidence Determination Excellence Honor Joyfulness Purposefulness Service Trustworthiness Truthfulness	Courage Creativity Enthusiasm Humility Patience Prayerfulness Self-Discipline Thankfulness
Justice/Unity Plane	
Assertiveness Compassion Gentleness Helpfulness Justice Loyalty Reliability Tact	Caring Forgiveness Friendliness Generosity Kindness Mercy Respect Tolerance Unity

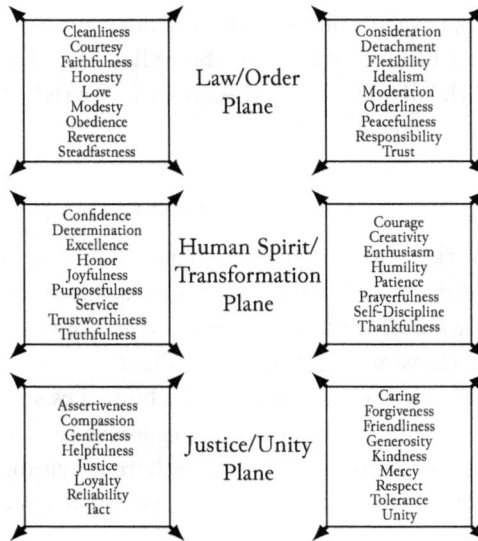

Diagram 4b: Six planes and fifty-two virtues

Good will is the renown a business acquires on account of past achievements. It implies the expectation that the bearer of the good will in the future will live up to his earlier standards. Good will is not a phenomenon appearing only in business relations. It is present in all social relations. It determines a person's choice of his spouse and of his friends and his voting for a candidate in elections. "Catallactics" [see quotation on the next page for a definition], of course, deals only with commercial good will.

It does not matter whether the good will is based on real achievements and merits or whether it is only a product of imagination and fallacious ideas. What counts in human action is not truth as it may appear to an omniscient being, but the opinions of people liable to error. There are some instances in which customers are prepared to pay a higher price for a special brand of a compound although the branded article does not differ in its physical and chemical structure from another cheaper product. Experts may deem such conduct unreasonable. But no man can acquire expertness in all fields which are relevant for his choices. He cannot entirely avoid substituting confidence in men for knowledge of the true state of affairs. The regular customer does not always select the article or the

service, but the purveyor whom he trusts. He pays a premium
to those whom he considers reliable."[12, pp. 379–80]

Restating that last point again, "He pays a premium to those whom
he considers reliable." Notice the clear assertion that a 'premium,'
a price, is ascribed to the practice of the virtue, in this case 'reliability.' In
other words, there is a commercial aspect to the virtue. It is a 'traceable'
market phenomenon.

> "Catallactics has accomplished its task only when it has suc-
> ceeded in this process of generalization, only when it has *traced*
> *the formation of prices back to the point where acting man makes*
> *his choice* and pronounces his decision: I prefer A to B.
>   However, economics also stops here. It does not go further
> back."[13, p. 221]

Who knows what advances in the social sciences will come in the
distant future, whether the limit for economics identified above by
Mises will always remain. But economics can advance beyond where
it is now by approaching the limit that Mises defined. That is the
objective of this book.

Virtues / Service Examples

Given the precedent that already exists in the economic literature and
following the example of Mises, I will proceed along similar lines. I will
begin to exercise the Divine Microeconomy Model© by selecting one
virtue per vantage point plane and then I will systematically look at the
economics taking place at the micro level, at the level of the individual.
Keep in mind the reciprocity and symmetry shown in Diagram 2i on
Page 21 between the virtues and service.

Example One—'Flexibility' in the Order Plane

Each of us knows that having flexibility as a part of the order of
things makes life much more enjoyable. Flexible order in our lives
makes it easier for us to adjust to changes—the inevitable changes that
occur in our lives.

Employers who provide an environment that incorporates flexibility
will tend to have a 'happier' workforce that most likely will translate

into a more productive and a more stable workforce. Also, customers appreciate having flexible and various options available to them if a product doesn't exactly meet their needs.

Flexibility incorporated into the production process—providing more options to employees and customers—leads to higher productivity and customer satisfaction, both of which are good for business.

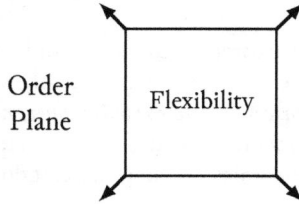

Order
Plane   Flexibility

Virtue Illustration 1: 'Flexibility' in the Order plane

Here we have customer satisfaction as one possible example of the 'tangible goods and services' emerging from flexibility.

Example Two—'Courtesy' in the Law Plane

No one is offended by being treated with courtesy. It inspires greater respect for oneself and, most definitely, greater respect for the courteous person.

Since the market is the embodiment of social cooperation, courtesies become the norm. If it is courteous to be on time that becomes the standard, 'out of courtesy.' And each time these courteous practices are applied the social relationships advance to new levels of mutual respect. As a consequence cooperation and coordination improves.

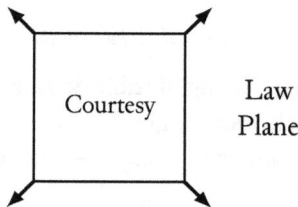

Courtesy   Law
                Plane

Virtue Illustration 2: 'Courtesy' in the Law plane

Here we have market cooperation and coordination as examples of the 'tangible goods and services' emerging from courtesy. By acquiring and practicing courtesy, work relationships will change and there will be a tremendous increase in productivity since cooperation and coordination will increase.

Example Three—'Excellence' in the Human Spirit Plane

As an expression of my will to live and love life, I show a particular keenness towards the things that I enjoy. It follows, then, that I will continue to strive for excellence in that pursuit, whatever it is.

Matching the right task with the right person to perform the task is one key to productivity and entrepreneurs are alert to this prospect. If those who are producing a good or service excel at it then everyone in the entire economy benefits, ultimately.

Imagine yourself having to choose between various products of similar prices but you happen to know that one company has a reputation for excellent production standards. This attribute is known as product quality and it is a major factor in decision-making. Of course you, as well as everyone else, will choose the best product.

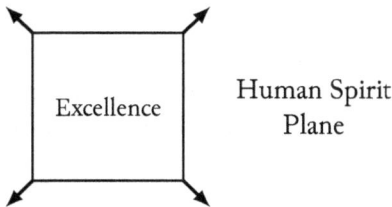

Virtue Illustration 3: 'Excellence' in the Human Spirit plane

Here we have product quality as an example of the 'tangible goods and services' emerging from excellence. By acquiring and practicing excellence there will be a more refined division of labor which will translate into greater productivity.

Example Four—'Patience' in the Transformation Plane

There is no way that everything can be understood instantaneously. Processing and understanding takes time. Those who are patient are known for their wisdom, a wisdom that partially comes from the practice of patience.

The same is true for production. It takes time. The goods and services that people want need to be generated and those who can envision and nurture the production process patiently over time render a great service.

Everyone can participate in this patience-requiring production process by exercising patience themselves—exhibited in their lives by saving. This saving and investment then converts into the much needed capital used in production processes, which can be seen as the economic equivalent to patience since capital represents goods for the future.

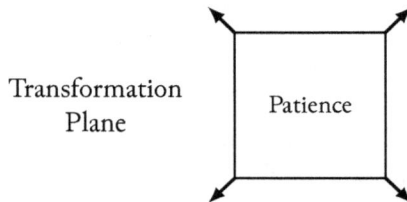

Transformation Plane   Patience

Virtue Illustration 4: 'Patience' in the Transformation plane

Here we have capital as an example of the 'tangible goods and services' emerging from patience. By acquiring and practicing patience, errors from short-sighted decisions will decrease and the savings necessary for economic growth will more likely be available.

Example Five—'Assertiveness' in the Justice Plane

Nobody can read your mind. If you take it upon yourself to make sure that others know what is important to you, then you can claim to be assertive.

The market is a dynamic process and it requires some assertive behavior to function properly. The alert entrepreneurs are actually assertive about the discrepancies that they find and they are assertive in applying their subsequent action.

It is this dispersal of knowledge that results from the actions taken by the entrepreneurs that keeps the whole system working and keeps knowledge flowing. Assertive and active entrepreneurs are, therefore, major contributors to the elimination of ignorance.

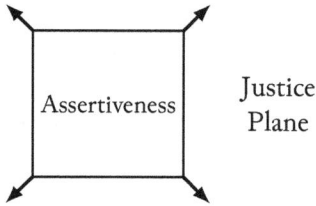

Virtue Illustration 5: 'Assertiveness' in the Justice plane

Here we have entrepreneurship as an example of the 'tangible goods and services' emerging from assertiveness. By acquiring and practicing assertiveness the speed and accuracy of the flow of knowledge will improve, leading to the discovery of more opportunities.

Example Six—'Mercy' in the Unity Plane

The world is a testing ground for our souls. Tests and difficulties exist and have to be dealt with.

How can we truly show that we care without a capacity for mercy? Those who feel blessed in plenteousness often show their feelings of mercy by contributing to or participating in some kind of charity. Charities channel peoples' mercy to those in need.

Mercy is one of the keys to prosperity. It is through the act of being merciful that one begins and continues to recognize the reasons to be thankful, and the act of being merciful also makes one feel prosperous. It is through mercy that those who are suffering are given their much needed sustenance which, too, is a prosperous feeling indeed.

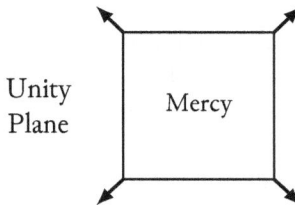

Virtue Illustration 6: 'Mercy' in the Unity plane

Here we have the feeling of prosperity as an example of the 'tangible goods and services' emerging from mercy. By acquiring and practicing mercy the extremes of wealth and poverty will lessen and a greater sense of prosperity will be felt by all. Those who show mercy will be recognized for this noble and valuable trait. A price, a 'premium' in some form, can be ascribed to the practice of 'mercy.' In other words, there is a commercial aspect to the virtue. It is a traceable market phenomenon.

The Art and Science of Economics

Notice, this is another duality! The way to bring together, in practice, the art and science of economics is to keep in mind the symmetry and reciprocity of all things, both the 'ideal' and the material.

It is the non-directional nature of both virtues and service which makes the microeconomy divine. Virtues lead to service and service leads to the acquisition of virtues. No matter where you are in this cycle—acquiring a virtue or applying the virtue in some type of service—there is a continuous potential for inspiration that further energizes the cycle.

It is the directional nature of cause and effect that makes the human being economic, always seeking the best means to attain the ends chosen.

It is the combination of both the non-directional and the directional natures of the microeconomy, blending them together as a human expression and experience, which constitutes the art and science of economics. It is, also, the recognition that both means and ends have the potential to be either 'ideal' or material which broadens the scope of praxeology and begins to bring about a merging of the art and science of economics.

Here are a couple of examples. Entrepreneurial alertness is interfered with by ignorance yet by definition it helps to alleviate ignorance. If a person who is prejudiced tries to serve as an entrepreneur, will that entrepreneur correctly be able to find all of the opportunities? Will the role of knowledge as defined in the divine economy be fully exercised? No, not fully.

Here is another example; virtues and service are highly valued. Even though they are 'ideal' they can and are given value. These ideal goods and services are assigned values in terms of the medium of exchange thus making them comparable to material goods and services.

The art and science of religion and economics merge when the medium of exchange is seen as a way to represent the value of the virtue. That is true whether the virtue is being exchanged for indirectly —because it is a part of the total product (most of the time)—or whether the virtue is directly the product. If I am trustworthy I will be compensated in some manner for possessing that quality as it finds integral ways to contribute to the production process. And perhaps I may even receive a direct payment, a tip for instance.

Of course the process of the divine microeconomy works positively on the minds and hearts of mankind. Progress begins the instant someone enters into the market process. Progress begins with the inevitable exposure to the flow of knowledge, which eventually leads to personal conviction, and then that newly acquired knowledge is put into practice.

This process has a pattern: new knowledge, conviction, and practice. Each step is remarkable and uniquely human.

The condition that must be met for each step to proceed is the same. The condition that must be met is the independent investigation of truth. As it turns out independent investigation of truth is not a difficult condition to be met, since it is simply a part of our human operating system. Learning how to learn is directly related to the ability to unleash this power. Alertness, awareness, and purposeful action are all a part of the process.

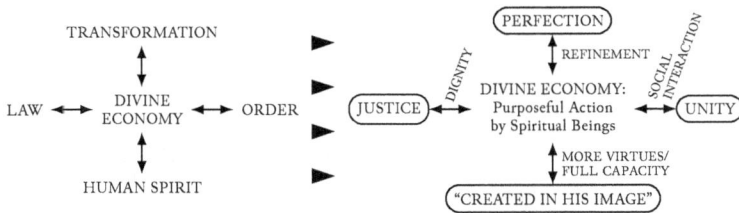

Skeletal Structure of the
Divine Economy Model©

The Divine Spark

Diagram 4c: Derivation from the skeletal structure of the Divine Economy Model all the way to the Divine Spark

Again we are talking about something that is dynamic and ever-changing. The divine spark is dynamic and ever-changing. Once ignited it takes on the quality of ardor. In the Divine Microeconomy Model © there are four incentives that intensify the ardor. These are: Justice, Perfection, Unity and "Created in the Image."

The omnipresent flint for the spark and the fuel for the ardor is purposeful action by spiritual beings. The economy exists because 'man' exists. The economy serves human existence. Its equilibrating power guarantees that it will fulfill its purpose.

As it turns out, individual virtues (the attributes of God) are at the heart of all actions. This process is dynamic, exciting, fulfilling, effective, inspiring and divine. As an art form the 'spark' has radial symmetry (one half is the mirror image of the other half) just like the human temple has radial symmetry.

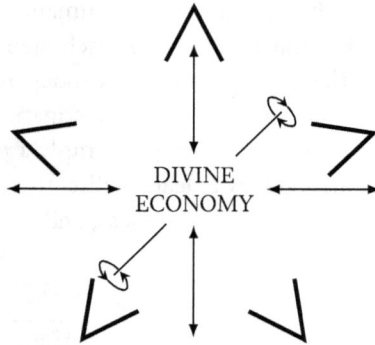

Diagram 4d: The symmetry of the Divine Spark

The spark, lying in potential in all human beings, is what leads to the manifestation of economic progress. It becomes manifest as purposeful action. The economy is the matrix where the flow of action becomes the flow of the grace and bounty of God, as depicted at the micro level in Diagram 4e.

Consider the complexity of this model. All these vantage point planes are actively in progress at the same time and all the virtues lying in those planes are more or less energized. The infinite scope of all of this resides within each individual from one moment to the next.

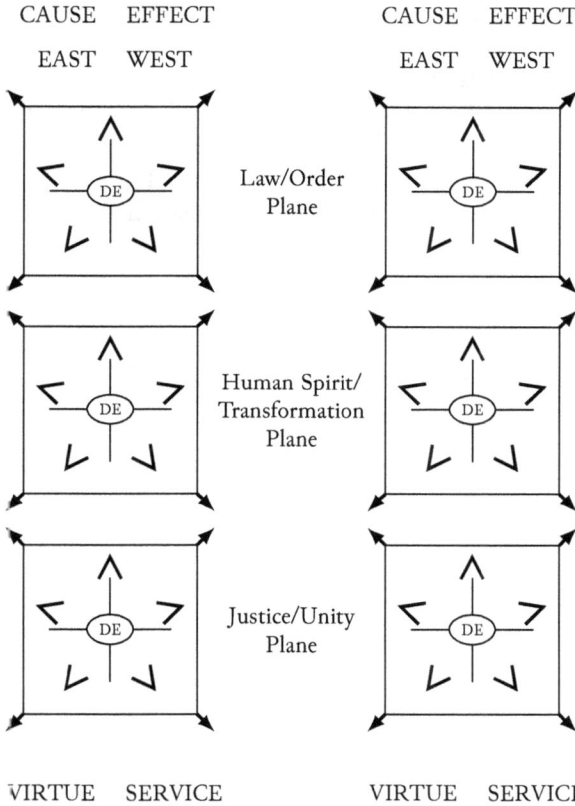

Diagram 4e: Divine Microeconomy Model with the Divine Spark

Then there are the inevitable encounters with others in the market process which further defines the divine economy. The complexity of the microeconomic model does not simply end there because these market encounters become a part of the market process which seamlessly extends across the time horizon and extends outward to affect everyone on the planet. In other words, at every instant the divine microeconomy is occurring within the divine economy. These simple yet complex models—the Divine Economy Model © and the Divine Microeconomy Model ©—attempt to portray this exquisite symphony.

Selected Exercises

1. Select a vantage point and find a virtue on the plane that you want to develop into a virtues/service example. Describe the economic applications and outcomes.

2. Spend some time examining Diagram 4c. How can you describe in your own words what makes the divine spark an important economic entity?

Chapter 5
Twill

Connectivity Between
Macroeconomics and Microeconomics

PREFACE

With the tapestry now unfolded and fully exposed it is not possible to fully appreciate it without spending time closely examining it and feeling its rich texture. There is a palpable depth to it, revealing yet another aspect of its marvelous complexity and artfulness. The texture of this tapestry is very much a perceptual treat which allows for new and different perspectives and further uncovers another layer of its overall complexity and connectivity, adding even more value and merit.

A SLIGHT DEMARCATION

What brings together the tapestry of economics as a whole—no matter which perspective it is that you are envisioning from—is its purpose. It is the study of the ways and means to attain the ends, whether the ends are societal or personal. Both means and ends are chosen subjectively in accordance with human nature.

The methodology of subjectivism gives us the power to discover new economic insights at the micro and macro levels. The same essential economic institutions serve as the foundation for both micro and macro considerations. These are: private property and private ownership of the means of production; savings and capital accumulation; the division of labor; voluntary exchange and money; financial self interest and the profit motive and economic competition; and the price system.

The market process is a required and necessary condition for the economy to even exist. The equilibrating power inherent in the divine economy will ultimately destroy any artificiality imposed on it. Quickly all intervention will be erased once the impetus ceases, with the market process re-emerging, purified and ready to go.

Across the entire horizon spans the economy. There is no distinct beginning or ending for the micro and macro portions since the economy is *entirely seamless.*

There are those in economics who have made distinctions and separated micro and macro in their artificial mental constructs. For instance the empiricist Irving Fisher in the 1920's claimed that price stability should be the macroeconomic goal (which is nothing more than price fixing when seen from the micro level)—which led to a bias against price deflation.

However, if prices go down it simply indicates that there is either greater productivity and/or a greater supply relative to the demand. This is a good thing, just like at the micro level where lower prices are desirable to you and me. This discrepancy between the micro level and the macro level promulgated by Fisher stands out as flawed logic. In other words, in the real world the economics at the level of micro and macro are always compatible and not at odds.

The deductive thought process that serves to identify the universal principles that operate holistically (macro) applies equally well at the level of the inspired acts of individuals (micro). There is however a small distinction that is detectable. Using deductive thinking, what may be better described as a 'fold line' rather than a 'seam' can be detected.

Microeconomics looks closely at the individual and the interaction of the individual with the market itself. Macroeconomics focuses on the market process and the market foundations.

MACROECONOMICS

What are the market foundations? To state it in broad terms: one, the desires of the populace are infinite; two, production is ultimately for consumption; three, production takes time; four, an increase in goods leads to an increase in the standard of living; and five, an increase in capital goods leads to a future increase in the standard of living. And finally, making exchanges—as in trading—is made possible by and leads to specialization and the division of labor.

The market process is a series of systematic changes in the inter-connected network of market decisions. It is where prices act as the signals and are used to put things together. It is this market process that serves to overcome imperfect knowledge and uncertainty. Prices emerging from the market are stepping stones through the unknown complexities of demand and supply.

In parallel, capital is like a bridge spanning the time horizon and the structure of that capital bridge is heterogeneous. It is heterogeneous in the sense that capital in the form of capital goods stretches all the way from savings through production, and continuing through distribution to the end points—which are the final goods and services. It is the profit-seeking entrepreneur who finds the ways and means to facilitate all of the cooperation that needs to happen in the economy for production to be successful across the time horizon.

Equally as important to understand, the market foundation has relevance because of purposeful human action and it rests upon property rights. By the design of the ego-driven interventionists the macroeconomic factors of capital, property rights, the market, and economic liberty receive the brunt of all of the economically harmful acts of intervention. Prosperity and peace suffer as a result of all intervention.

Economic intervention begins at the macro level and it trickles its way to the micro level and is very disruptive at both the macro and micro level. Interventionism starts at the macro level by interfering with the processes that bring order, or by obstructing the transformation processes. Not only that but laws are converted into legal codes for easy manipulation, and the attempt is to collectivize the human spirit when the economy is subjected to interventionism. These are all corruptions.

Artificially dissecting the economy into macro and micro is what makes interventionism possible. It follows the strategic plan of attack by the ego-driven enemy: divide and conquer! But macro and micro are one whole, inseparable. Separating them is a corruption.

Macro/Micro

What does it mean that the divine economy is seamless? Replying succinctly—the equilibrating power is always in operation throughout the economy, at both the micro and macro level.

Another way to answer the question is to recognize that there are no internal disciplines, no fields or subfields. There is no abstract separation from historical events or from politics; they are all happening within the economy. Nor is there a time zone where you enter the long run 'time zone' and leave the short run 'time zone.' It is an all-inclusive continuum.

Since the economy is one whole, there are no non-integrated portions exclusively studied by 'experts' that require special tools or devices. Praxeology, a general theory of human action, is the universal tool that can be applied by novice or master to understand the economy.

Playfully though, we will entertain ourselves by trying to discover the distinctions between micro and macro! Microeconomics focuses its attention on profit and loss by focusing on prices whereas macroeconomics broadens that view to look at the role of money as a medium and facilitator of exchange. Demand is a function of purchasing power and purchasing power is supposed to be a function of money. Calculation of profit and loss in each successive short run contributes to the functioning of the market process, which in the long run manifests itself as economic growth. So macroeconomics seems to be about the long run and about business cycles.

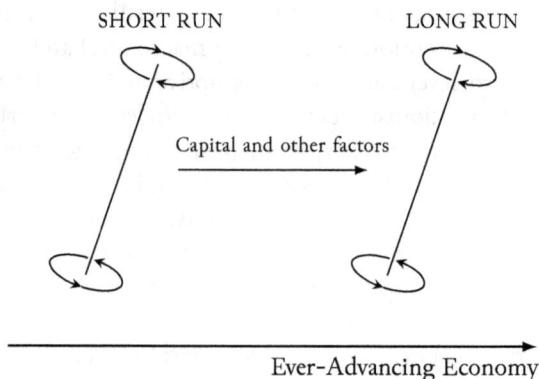

SHORT RUN   LONG RUN

Capital and other factors
→

Ever-Advancing Economy

Diagram 5a: Economic Growth

Graphically translated we can represent economic growth and the long run as movement to the right of the axis of the nature and role of knowledge, as depicted in Diagram 5a. We can also graphically represent the long run (notice that it is movement to the left) that occurs as a result of an intervention-induced business cycle, as depicted in Diagram 5b. These two diagrams are very similar to and derived from Diagram 4t which originally appeared in *More than Laissez-Faire*[6, p. 71].

Referred to as the Business Cycle

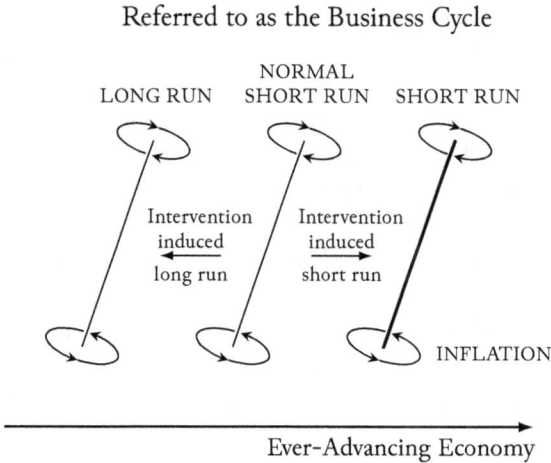

Diagram 5b: Hampered long-run economic growth

Notice in Diagram 5b that the consequences of intervention in the short run from the macro viewpoint may seem rosy but ultimately the long run economic growth ends up being hampered (when the bubble bursts). From the microeconomic viewpoint the trickle down effects of economic intervention are also destructive. As an example, when the money supply is increased it causes the purchasing power of money to decline. This is what makes nominal prices higher than real prices, which means that nominal total revenues are higher than real total revenues. Profits, necessarily, will be overestimated.

Now combine that with the effect on capital over time. Estimates used to decide whether production is a viable option will be distorted since the purchasing power of money will unforeseeably decline. Capital will not be accurately depreciated and the return on investment in the form of paying factors of production now for an investment return later will be less than expected since the money will be worth less in the future.

Additionally economic intervention in the monetary system makes the banking system inherently fraudulent and insolvent. In a centralized banking system it is through the banks that the inflated money enters and circulates. It is through the banks that the money supply is further inflated in a fractional reserve banking system.

In this way all sources of credit—from banks and also capital from firms and individuals—are subjected to theft due to the diminishing purchasing power of the money at pay back time. Business calculations are distorted—profits and returns on investments are overestimated, costs are underestimated—contracts are rendered increasingly meaningless and the ethics of the whole system fizzles out. As you can see human civilization recedes rather than advances as a result of intervention. Intervention causes the standard of living to decline. In this case the example of intervention was inflation of the money supply.

One definition of macroeconomics that then emerges is as follows: **it is a study of those factors and conditions that lead to the long run advancement of the standard of living for everyone on the planet.** By definition, then, economic intervention is bad economics.

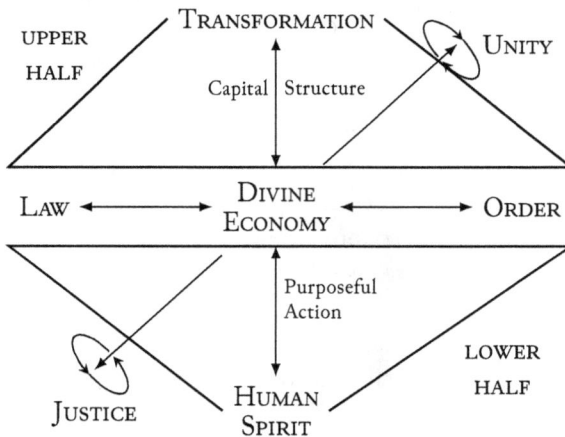

Diagram 5c: Macro and micro tendencies seen in the Divine Economy Model ©

Another playful representation of the distinction between micro and macro looks a little closer at the upper half and the lower half of the Divine Economy Model ©. Examine Diagram 5c and you will see that the upper half seems to 'speak of' macroeconomics while the lower half 'speaks of' microeconomics.

Notice the upper triangle (macro portion) of transformation, law and order shares its base with the lower triangle (micro portion) of human spirit, law and order. Sharing the same base tends to blur the distinction between micro and macro—true to reality. In other words, the divine economy is seamless!

Regarding the upper half, the capital structure is a principal intermediary element in the model and it brings about transformation. Since capital is a significant feature of the long run time horizon the upper half has strong macroeconomic characteristics. Regarding the lower half, the human-spirit-motivated purposeful action is a principal intermediary element in the model, giving a strong indication that it is the microeconomic level of the individual—as a consumer, a producer, a resource owner, an entrepreneur, a capitalist, or part and parcel of some of each—that is being represented.

Microeconomics

There is not much need to go into this since it was covered in detail in Chapters 3 and 4. Suffice it to say that for the individual, each interaction with the economy is a learning experience. Each experience in the series of market interactions—that are necessarily a part of life—leads to a furtherance of knowledge.

One definition of microeconomics that then emerges is as follows: **it is a study of how individuals discover and react to information in the market as part of their division of labor to produce and to earn income, so as to meet their personal desires for goods and services.**

Each experience in the series of knowledge gaining experiences is more competitive than the preceding period. In other words, we are constantly searching for ways to make things better for ourselves. And since competition and entrepreneurship are analytically inseparable these experiences act to stimulate our entrepreneurship. That is very good news indeed since releasing our potential, by changing our entrepreneurship from latent to active, leads to prosperity.

❖

Selected Exercises

1. Use yourself as an analogy! Assume your personality is the microeconomy and your life is the macroeconomy. Comment on the empirical economists' attempts to separate the two.

2. Notice the horizontal 'fold line' in Diagram 5c. Even though there is no real separation what insights do you have after considering the definitions of microeconomics and macroeconomics given in this chapter?

Chapter 6
Potency of the Essence

The Praxeology of Entrepreneurship

PREFACE

What is the cause of the volatility of the olfactory elements within the essence? There is some activation that occurs due to the clashing between elemental factors and the environment. Whatever it is, the activator makes everything else about the essence—its true qualities and nature—come bursting into existence. The essence would be devoid of its true reality without the activator.

THE ESSENCE OF ENTREPRENEURSHIP

The *praxeology* of *entrepreneurship*! Hold on to your hats! These are two very powerful words! An alternative description for this chapter is—Entrepreneurship: The Premier Fruit for the Study of Human Action.

First we need to understand praxeology. It is the study of human action logic. It is action logic that takes into account time and causality. It is logic action in the passage of time. The notable characteristics of praxeology are time and causality and human action.

What emerges from this reflection is the consideration of the difference between a priori and a posteriori reasoning. A priori is from cause to effect, is based on something known—such as natural law—and it is valid independently of observation. A posteriori is based upon actual observation or upon experimental data, starting there and working back to their causes. Speaking about the power of science and the power of appropriate methodology, Mises says: "What makes natural science possible is the power to experiment, what makes social science possible is the power to grasp or to comprehend the meaning of human action."[11, ch. 1, section III]

Understanding human action is the goal of social science. Embedded, implied in human action is the learning process. Just like the ultimate competitor faced by an athlete is his own self or her own self, the learning process is competitive, with each learning experience topping the previous understanding.

Praxeology studies the form and the structure of human action. Human action occurs in the worldly condition of radical uncertainty. The urge to act is irrepressible, yet because of the uncertainty the consequences of the action are not known. This is part of the human condition—we act purposefully in an uncertain world.

Homo agens—us—we are endowed with the propensity for alertness toward fresh goals and the discovery of as yet unknown resources. This is the perfect complement to the matrix of our world, a world composed of uncertainty and imperfect knowledge. From this matrix, through the channel of alert human action, comes entrepreneurship.

If the economy ever reached a sustainable equilibrium there would be no need for alertness. But the real world is dynamically in disequilibrium, perpetually driven towards equilibrium. Alertness therefore is a main ingredient. This human propensity towards alertness shows up in two ways. Goals are pursued efficiently in a constant search to find the following: 1) which ends to pursue, and 2) which means are available.

Alertness is the entrepreneurial element in human decision-making. Now it is "possible to explain the pattern of change in an individual's decisions as the outcome of a learning process generated by the unfolding experience from the decisions themselves."[5, p. 36] Decisions are made based on what was learned from previous decisions.

The keys to understanding entrepreneurship are that the entrepreneur discovers opportunities, responds to opportunities and generates opportunities by bearing uncertainty. This process is a competitive process which exists when there is freedom; freedom for those with better ideas to pursue their ideas, and freedom for those with a greater willingness to serve to then go ahead and serve the needs conveyed via the market process.

As a result of competitive entrepreneurship the movement of the 'knowledge axis' is to the right, as shown in Diagram 6a, which is in the 'ever-advancing' direction and which can be attributed to the human propensity for alertness.

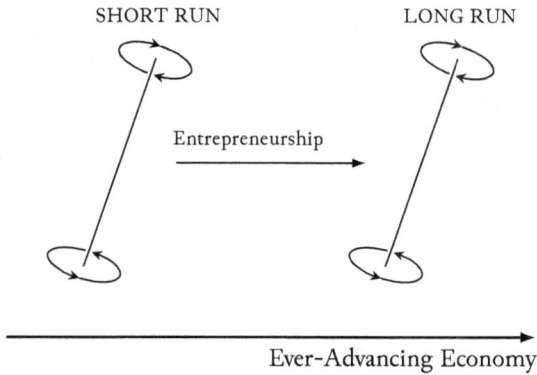

SHORT RUN   LONG RUN

Entrepreneurship

Ever-Advancing Economy

Diagram 6a: Entrepreneurship moves the knowledge axis to the right

Successful identification of the relevant ends and means is what ultimately determines whether a decision is right. If it is 'right' the axis moves to the right! The advancement of the market process and of the divine economy and of civilization is the motive; albeit hidden deep within the human reality.

There is no way to separate alertness from the competitive environment since they are parts of the same process. Superior awareness is the natural mode of operation and is potentially striven for by everyone.

Since the entrepreneur acts upon the economy, the entrepreneur is part of its dynamic character. This ever-changing character of the economy makes instantly obsolete any attempt to view the economy as static. What enables the subjective methodology to incorporate the instantly ever-changing economy into theory is the emphasis it gives to the praxeology of entrepreneurship.

FORM OF ENTREPRENEURSHIP

The first part of our praxeological study of entrepreneurship will look at its form. The action of entrepreneurs drives forward the tendency towards equilibrium and it generates a process which is competitive by nature.

It is truly competitive. One bit of evidence confirming this is the existence of purely entrepreneurial activity, pure arbitrage, which requires no resource ownership. In other words, there is no barrier to entry into the market since alertness is the only requirement. In this dimension of pure entrepreneurial activity the discovery of a profit opportunity represents the discovery of something for nothing at all.

Why are there unnoticed opportunities? One reason—imperfect knowledge. For example, resource owners and consumers are often passive in the very dynamic economy. What 'unnoticed opportunities' means is that there will necessarily be more efficient ways to coordinate transactions in the resource and product market. Whoever steps forward as an entrepreneur and bears the uncertainty inherent in the market will be the one who is in the position to capture these opportunities.

Moment to moment any market participant can become an entrepreneur or not, either now or later, or over and over again. And even though economic roles are multiple—yet still they are distinct. For instance, resource ownership and entrepreneurship are completely separate functions; nevertheless the same person may be an entrepreneur, a resource owner and a capitalist and yet still perform these functions independently.

It is in the competitive market where the entrepreneur plays a critical role. Paradoxically, as it happens, the market process is competitive because it is entrepreneurial. Market information is acquired through the experience of market participation. And entrepreneurial action is taken in response to the changes that occur in the market data, assuming that the changes are detected. So it is that prospective decisions of buyers and sellers at every step in the production process are subjected to this competitively alert scrutiny.

The entrepreneur discovers a profit opportunity when the prices of products somewhere in the production process are not properly adjusted to the prices of the resource services in the factor markets. A keen eye for assessing the marginal value product of each factor, relative to the final price of the good consumed, helps the entrepreneur determine whether its 'productive share' is undervalued (or overvalued).

Lower prices, higher quality, and more products to choose from are what people want so entrepreneurs are also striving for these and deserve the credit for bringing them about. Along the way the profit seeking entrepreneur brings about new cooperative arrangements between previously disconnected parties. For example, resource owners may be made aware of a profit opportunity and then decide to take on the role of a capitalist. Another example, as a result of entrepreneurial discovery producers may begin working with new resource owners or they may begin producing for a different group of consumers.

Before leaving the examination of entrepreneurial form let us reconsider the fact that resource owners and consumers are often passive. They act as if the prices they see are 'equilibrium' prices. These errors yield opportunities for profitable activity.

'Enter the producers!' since they are never immune from competition. They inevitably and significantly take on the role of entrepreneur. The drive for producing the best products at the lowest prices, subject to competitive pressures, makes the producer a natural candidate for keen alertness.

STRUCTURE OF ENTREPRENEURSHIP

To examine the structure of entrepreneurship we will combine its form with the price system. If there ever appears to be a lull in entrepreneurial activities—and there happens to be no intervention—it simply means that the market participants have not yet become aware of the opportunities or are not willing to bear the uncertainties that are there. However, competitive entrepreneurship guarantees that the discovery and pursuit of the opportunities is on the near horizon.

Market participants will allocate resources to the investments with the highest present value and then to the next highest, successively, discounting the expected future value. In the real world economy this reckoning of the time horizon is of great importance. In a world like we have nowadays, most production processes are time consuming which means that entrepreneurial profit opportunities typically require capital, so it is that, capital is part of the entrepreneurial structure.

What is the nature of the forces that bring about changes in the existing market patterns? It is the successful identification of relevant ends and means.

With the goal being to successfully sell the product; all the costs incurred by the entrepreneur are for this purpose. This differs from 'pure' arbitrage in that input prices attributed to resource ownership precede output sales. In this production process the entrepreneur 'guesses' that the future product price—the market price or the selling price—is not fully synchronized with today's input prices. It is an educated guess, a risk, since the product prices do not exist at the time production begins. If the assessment proves true, this is what causes profits to emerge since the astute entrepreneur will have judged the future prices correctly across the time horizon.

The keen entrepreneur is able to forecast demand and costs in the competitive environment of the market. Very often entrepreneurs use capital to pay workers now and then reap a profit later. The competitive market ensures that those who are most able to satisfy the consumers' desires earn the greatest profits, which means that the most adept entrepreneurs will always be the ones serving the consumers. This selection process benefits everyone.

Part of this structure, maintained by the entrepreneur, goes beyond the actual good produced. In the real world, the entrepreneur/producer assists the sometimes latent consumer by extending the umbrella of alertness. Their selling effort reaches out to potential consumers, trying to activate their alertness by persuasion (attempting to change consumers' tastes) and by providing them with information about purchase opportunities. Likewise the umbrella of alertness, directly attributed to the entrepreneur, is extended to the resource owners and to the capitalists.

If a monopoly exists in any degree, independent of the artificial forms caused by intervention, it is because of resource ownership control. A monopoly simply cannot exist—because of the powerful dissecting force of competitive entrepreneurship—unless there is restricted access to needed resources which blocks potential entrepreneurs from discovering any of those unexploited opportunities for profit. Nevertheless even the monopoly position of a resource owner is always under intense competition and there is pressure to use the resource in the most efficient manner. A monopoly can only exist in the long run by protective intervention. If a monopoly is said to have a 'structure' then competitive entrepreneurship is the antithesis of that type of structure.

ENTREPRENEURSHIP AND THE FIRM

A detailed analysis of the firm is beyond the scope of this book but the survival of the firm, assuming there is no artificial support of the firm by way of intervention, depends on the nurturing of the spirit of entrepreneurship. The starting point is recognition that a firm is a complex entity.

Firms emerge. Owners of productive resources sell their services to the firm, to be used to satisfy the 'cries' of the consumer. It is those who are entrepreneurial, hearing the cries and seeing the opportunities and bearing the uncertainty, who originate the firm and who keep it viable.

Inside the firm there is a structure within which reward and punishment operates in all of its subtleties. Unlike with an individual the firm may have internal layers that move the productive efforts of the individuals away from direct interaction with market prices. Within the firm the incentive and disincentive strategy may or may not be reflective of the real world market. The further away the incentive/disincentive strategy of the firm is from the real world market the more likely there will be errors that will ultimately affect the viability of the firm.

And so it is necessary for the firm to create a culture of entrepreneurship in such a way that there are ties to the market process ideally at every locus of decision/action. Alertness must include detecting the closeness to market prices and discovering ways to stay close. If a firm has this as its goal it will inherently be innovative and a source of bounty for those within the firm. At the same time this kind of firm will be able to render service optimally to those people who desire what the firm has to offer.

If for legal reasons the firm takes on a corporate form, its goal—compatible with competitive entrepreneurship—is to put the resources to work "in the most lucrative way known to the relevant decision-makers."[5, p. 63] Regardless of what the form happens to be this entrepreneurial selection of the business form is also a part upon which the viability of the firm rests.

Corporate decision-makers, managers, act as true entrepreneurs only to the extent that the entrepreneurial opportunities detected translate into personal benefit. Without this type of arrangement the full potential of the market process is wasted, untapped because the entrepreneurial potential is limited.

How could it not be limited? It is the incentivized entrepreneur who will seek to know who to hire and it is the incentivized entrepreneur who will seek to know where to find the market information that reveals profit opportunities. Also, it is the entrepreneur who will leave if the firm undervalues his or her services.

If the management is entrepreneurial it experiences the same forces of competitive entrepreneurship as everyone else, which necessarily leads to accountability. When a corporation moves away from this ideal then a different structure appears. If the stockholders lack the effective power to fire management the corporation takes on a degree of monopoly structure due to the incumbency of the manager. The management lacks accountability and is sheltering itself from the competitive entrepreneurship inherent in the divine economy.

Implied in the divine economy is the existence of pure entrepreneurial activity where price discrepancies throughout are detected and acted upon and where there are no obstacles to freedom of entry. Eventually these forces of competitive entrepreneurship will dissect and dismantle all firms that ignore what it is that drives the economy forward; and that is competitive entrepreneurship.

◈

Selected Exercises

1. How does your understanding of prosperity change when you realize that pure entrepreneurship is the discovery of something for nothing at all?

2. How does entrepreneurship serve the consumers and how does it serve everyone in the production process?

3. What are some ways that strategies used internally within the firm can be made to be entrepreneurial?

Chapter 7
The Beauty of the Tapestry

Entrepreneurship and Human Virtues

PREFACE

Almost forgotten is the artistic panorama which unfolds as the beautiful tapestry is laid out completely. Apart from all of the intricacies of the tapestry as a piece of art that has practical uses, it is also a very real expression of human creativity and action. It incorporates and represents knowledge, volition, and action—within itself—which is the pinnacle of human existence. It symbolizes the goodness of human action.

DISCOVERY OF THE VALUE AND PURPOSE OF ENTREPRENEURSHIP

In the introduction to this book on page 3 I wrote the following: "This inherent drive is all about being *alert*. Seen in this way it is evident that even entrepreneurship is essentially an exercise of a part of our *spiritual reality*. Those who exhibit praiseworthy characteristics will be found. And it is the desirability of *human virtues* that will continually move human civilization towards *prosperity*."

It is from this statement that the structure of this chapter is mirrored. Alertness, being an essence of our spiritual reality, makes us keenly aware of the human virtues which civilize us and make us prosperous. Although never perfected the changes and advancements along these lines lead to our refinement as individuals which then translates into an ever-advancing civilization with an ethical foundation. This is a classic example of cause and effect.

CAUSE   EFFECT   CAUSE   EFFECT

EAST   WEST   EAST   WEST

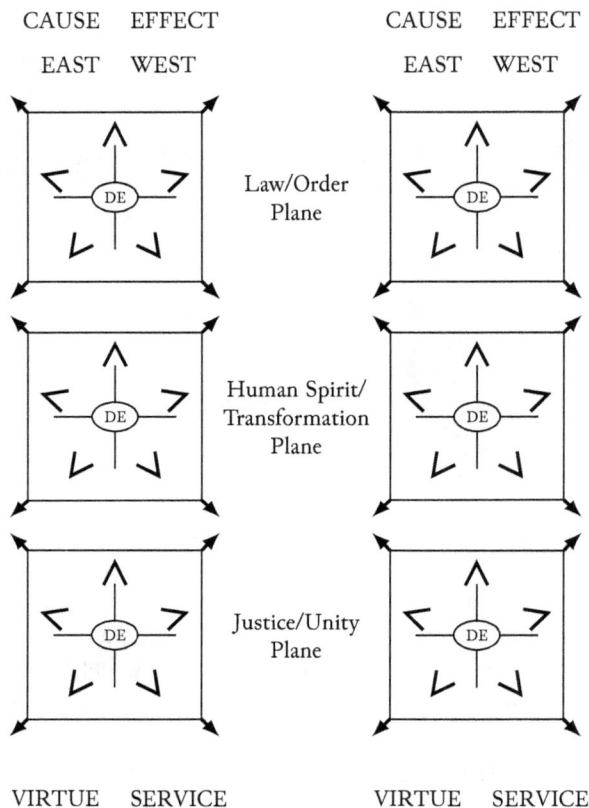

Law/Order
Plane

Human Spirit/
Transformation
Plane

Justice/Unity
Plane

VIRTUE   SERVICE   VIRTUE   SERVICE

Diagram 7a: Classic example of cause and effect: entrepreneurial spark throughout the Divine Microeconomy Tapestry

ALERTNESS AND THE HUMAN SPIRIT AND TRANSFORMATION

Looking from an entrepreneurial vantage point it is obvious that the
expression of wants is not only natural but it is also communicative.
Perpetual changes are always a feature of the economy, a part of the mix,
and those who are alert and active are energized, spreading knowledge
to others.

Since imperfect knowledge is the normal state of affairs, the ones
acting as discoverers across the time horizon forge themselves and
others into new and transformed individuals. There is a new balance

that is brought about by the information about reality that is sought after, and this new equilibrium tendency influences everyone.

This dynamic is happening in countless loci, from unique individuals all striving for betterment, which then affects everything in the surroundings. Many of the opportunities that present themselves do not go unnoticed since our propensity for alertness is inherent.

So, from this constant flow of information in the real world matrix of imperfect knowledge and uncertainty gems are noticed. Patterns of discovery are learned and all of this is used to inspire and transform ones' selves and others.

Law and Order of Spiritual Reality

It is the wonder of discovery that stimulates the potent and sometimes latent act of perception. What is especially enticing about the discovery is the possibility—that from what appears to be nothing something emerges. This is the quest 'to become' and this urge is part of the human operating system.

Inseparable is this quest from the desire for betterment. These combine to enhance the level of awareness and these operate within an individual and then overflow, affecting others. It is not something that ever comes to an end since we are finite in a world of infinite scope. Yet each discovery is a coordinating step that facilitates progress.

The search, high and low, culminates in action that indicates that a discovery is made. Then a new equilibrium tendency comes into existence with new transformation potentials which then gives new meaning to any subsequent human action.

The process is obviously evolutionary and stimulative. This is a process that releases our potential, changing our entrepreneurship from relatively latent to relatively active and the end result is relative prosperity. It is not something that can be helped—it is simply part of the human reality. In the worldly condition of radical uncertainty the urge to act is irrepressible. The motive hidden deep within the human reality is advancement.

If the learning process is successful then right decisions are made along the way. In other words, the alertness characteristic of the entrepreneurial spirit is the guide used to discover which ends to pursue and which means are available.

UNITY OF HUMAN VIRTUES

That is what is so unifying about human virtues. They are both an ends and a means. And not only that, the source of all value is traced back to them! This potency—having supreme distinction as a means, as an ends, and as the source of all value—is unique and it merits further consideration of yet another 'unity' distinction.

Human virtues 'bring together as a whole' the means, the ends, and economic value. Wow! And since there is nothing else that accomplishes this, another remarkable 'unity' distinction applies: *single and alone* it pulls together the ends (ethics), value, and the means (economics). Ethics and economics are brought together by human virtues!

Consequently, when the entrepreneurial spirit focuses its alertness on the appearance and the acquisition of human virtues there is a completeness that is unparalleled by any other act. Those who are truly entrepreneurial will recognize the importance of this and put it into practice which will then begin to transform and spiritualize the whole process.

PROSPERITY AND JUSTICE

And that entrepreneurial recognition and subsequent practice is what puts into effect the virtues-to-service cycles that are better known as prosperity! In this microeconomic matrix called the divine microeconomy, we are exploring a new twist on how economic life works. Regardless of any of the points of power and any of the essential realities, it is the entrepreneur who activates the powers in the economy like a spark ignites a flame.

Out of latency the alert ones connect the human desires and aspirations with those things that are needed to satisfy those needs and this is the source of prosperity. In other words, prosperity itself is latent and the entrepreneur is the one who is active in raising and creating an awareness that then propels the process forward.

As ends and means, the virtues permeate all things in the present and the future and it is the entrepreneur who helps to show how virtues are imputed throughout the economy and across the time horizon. This newly awakened awareness makes it possible for the individual actors in the economy to discern that the marginal value product of each factor is a function of how much it has contributed to the infusion into the final good or service the attributes of God, the virtues. It is this which makes it a 'good.'

Prosperity is our birthright. It is latent in us. That is where pure entrepreneurship comes in since it represents the discovery of something for nothing. Discovery of true value all around us requires only awareness!

It is the ends and the more roundabout means that are not at the immediate fingertips of the entrepreneur. But these are highly valued and so capital will be readily applied ordinally as soon as it is available for all the heterogeneous endeavors that are needed to meet the temporal needs of all of the diverse and subjective individuals in the world.

The entrepreneur is the principal catalyst that facilitates all of the cooperation that needs to happen in the economy across the time horizon. This is the glorious station of the entrepreneur! The increase in virtues and in services that translates into prosperity is brought about by alertness and is a wonderful expression and manifestation of justice.

To better understand what I mean by justice I refer you to what I said on page 70 about entrepreneurship and freedom:

"A key to understanding entrepreneurship is that the entrepreneur does not generate opportunities, but rather, responds to opportunities. This process is a competitive process which exists when there is freedom; freedom for those with better ideas to pursue their ideas, and freedom for those with a greater willingness to serve to then go ahead and serve the needs conveyed, via the market process."

✦

Selected Exercises

1. Based on what you read in this chapter what would you say is the significance of 'seeing' from an entrepreneurial vantage point?

2. What is the relationship between entrepreneurship and prosperity?

Epilogue:
Enriched by the Gift!

Adornment

PREFACE

Is there any reason to fragment the gift, or was the intention to confer as a whole both the potent essence and the tapestry? No doubt the gift was (and is) indivisible, intricate, exquisite, and purposeful. And it is the cause of great contentment!

ECONOMIC LIBERTY

Consider this shocking statement: one of the greatest tragedies of modern times is the association of economics with profit maximization and with efficiency! It is not that the concepts of profit maximization or efficiency cannot be simply understood in a different way, in a broader manner, but that is not what has happened. Instead, profit maximization and efficiency were defined narrowly and literally by empirical economists for the purpose of rationalizing their methodology.

I do not follow them down their road—a road that leaves behind the subjective nature of human beings—and I am not alone. Instead I take the path that honors the human reality—the path of subjectivism. This is a path with the rich heritage of classical liberalism which extends back centuries and which promises to extend well into the future. This classical liberalism tradition is rich with contributions from many different people over a long period of time. And it is also a very great tradition, with some exceedingly brilliant contributors to this valuable and notable heritage.

In a nutshell, classical liberalism provides an easy transition from the subjective nature of human beings to the economy and back again. What comes to the surface from using this classical liberalism approach, and its application of the subjective methodology, is a wealth of universal laws that pertain to human action. These laws then serve as the foundation for economics. 'Just like that' humans—not some imaginary creatures that fit equations—are the most important and yet still the most elusive part of the economy.

In subjectivism the economic world that the human faces is 'permitted' to be the actual real world, and the fact that it is always in disequilibrium is 'allowed.' Rather than trying to force everything into a ceteris paribus box to remove the real world conditions, subjectivism explores the real world as it 'operates' which leads to an understanding of the human processes of thought and action.

But not all thought and action pertain to material things. The 'ideal' and perhaps physically invisible things sought after, and applied, are nevertheless real to us—we who are the wonderful and great creatures known as human beings. Only the subjectivist methodology can penetrate into these largely unexplored, qualitative realms. That is what science is supposed to do, to penetrate the unknown, discovering new things.

I started this epilogue speaking about a modern tragedy. It is an exercise of ignorance to blame the economy for the ills facing mankind. The economy is a divine institution that brings the grace and bounty of God if we do not work against it. It is the vehicle for the expression of every person on the planet and a way for their unique talents and faculties to become known and to develop.

And at its most personal level—the microeconomy—this is where the attributes inherent in human beings can charge the world with goodness. The virtues and services that are the expressions of the motive force to act have been passed over and left out as economic realities, left out there somewhere in the oblivion of neglect, until now. Now they are tied tightly to the economic realities with the strong cord of economic science.

A new day is here and the horizon of subjectivism shines very bright indeed. Simply put, there is a spiritual solution to the economic problems. Subjectivism provides the bridge for understanding the economics of the solutions, thus bringing economic science and religion into harmony.

Finally, since the flow of knowledge is the great force affecting the market process it follows that anything that interferes with the flow of knowledge slows the process. This retarding of prosperity affects the divine economy at the macro level and also at the very personal micro level. Acts of intervention distort and disrupt the flow of knowledge. At the level of the individual the intervention-induced distortions may cause a person to act greedily instead of with moderation or it may cause a person to impatiently spend rather than wisely save.

Do you see what I am saying? The ills that we easily recognize as ills and which have been incorrectly attributed to the economy (I just mentioned greed and excessive consumption) can now be correctly attributed to their true source—the distortions that come from the acts of ego-driven interventionists. Intervention (acts imposed from outside the market process and that prevent the free flow of accurate information); it is this intervention that distorts and corrupts the microeconomy and the macroeconomy.

Intervention is like a veil that prevents us from recognizing that the economy is divine. With this book I have attempted and hopefully succeeded in lifting that veil! Even better, together let's work to tear asunder the veil of intervention by vehemently objecting to intervention at all levels and in all forms so that the countenance of the divine economy can beam its glory.

Finally, do not relinquish the responsibility of your own self—your human essence—to another, to someone else. The human *essence* of economics *essentially* is for each person to find their *essence*, and to polish it as a gem, and in this way attain wealth and bring about prosperity.

Glossary

A posteriori: Reasoning from observed facts or events back to their causes.

A priori: Working from something that is already known or self-evident to arrive at a conclusion

Arbitrage: Buying and selling to take advantage of discrepancies in the price of a good.

Capital: The financial resources which are necessary for the production of most current goods and all future goods.

Catallactics: The analysis of those actions which are conducted on the basis of monetary calculations.

Competitive entrepreneurship: The inherent alertness that fascinates and motivates human action in the real world condition of scarcity of time and means.

Consumer demand theory of value: Value and demand ultimately come from the consumer.

Contemporary price theory: Economic analysis based on the assumption of equilibrium.

Demand: The expression of wants using income from production.

Derived demand: Demand for all factors of production is derived from the demand for the final good.

Disequilibrium: The real economic condition that exists in the world because of uncertainty and imperfect knowledge.

Divine Economy: The equilibrium force that is at the center of the divine institution—the economy—that has been bestowed upon humankind by God.

Divine Economy Model: A subjectivist model that describes the economy in the following terms: human spirit, transformation, law, order, purposeful action, capital structure, market, property rights, justice, and unity.

Divine Economy Theory: The theory that uses the subjectivist methodology to explore how the human identity of being created in the 'image of God' helps us to understand how the economy works.

Divine Microeconomy Model©: A model that uses the subjectivist methodology to trace value back to its source and then opens new vistas for microeconomic exploration.

Divine spark: The irresistible tendency for humans to search for the truth that manifests itself as competitive entrepreneurship.

Division of labor: Since every human being is unique, as they pursue their goals there is the potential that they will make a unique contribution to production.

Dualism: A state in which something has two distinct parts or aspects, which are often opposites.

Empiricism: The use of data rather than theory to explain things.

Entrepreneur: The agent that is the driving force in the economy because of the exercising of alertness and the bearing of uncertainty.

Epistemology: The branch of philosophy that studies the nature of knowledge, in particular its foundations, scope, and validity

Equilibrium: The tendency towards balance and harmony.

Ever-advancing civilization: Humans, individually and as a whole, always aspire towards and potentially achieve greater perfections.

Ex ante: Before the event.

Ex post: After the fact.

Hampered Economy: This is an economy where acts of intervention interfere with the equilibrium forces.

Homo agens: He or she who exercises human action.

Human Operating System: All of the inherent human faculties that serve as the means to fulfill our human purpose, which ultimately is to know and love God.

Income: Purchasing power that results from production.

Inflation: Artificial expansion of the money supply.

Intervention: Acts imposed from outside the market process and that prevent the free flow of accurate information.

Laissez-faire: An economic philosophy based on the insight that the economy works best when there is no intervention.

Latent Entrepreneurship: A state of potential unachieved due to discernment dormancy.

Leisure: The desire to satisfy one's highest valued physical, intellectual, or spiritual aspiration instead of working.

Loss: Occurs when marginal costs are greater than marginal revenues.

Macroeconomy: A term used to indicate that aggregate indicators in the economy are being looked at.

Market: The place and process where information flows between and among participants.

Market clearing price: The price where the quantity demanded of a good will match what is supplied during that production cycle.

Market Process: A natural and universal process that functions like language does to facilitate, in this case, in the making of exchanges.

Methodological dualism: No bridge connects the external world of physical, chemical, and physiological phenomena and the internal world of human thought, feeling, valuation, and purposeful action.

NTA (Next Time Around): Production for the next planned sales period based on information and knowledge gained from the previous planned sales period.

PSP (Planned Sales Period): That period of time by the end of which the firm expects to sell out of the quantity supplied to the market.

Praxeology: The study of purposeful human action taken by spiritual beings.

Price: Information conveyed during the market process about the exchange value of a good.

Price elasticity: The degree of change in the quantity demanded if the price changes.

Production: The creation of useful goods and services.

Profit: The motivation that stimulates producers to increasingly meet the needs of the consumer thereby serving as an agent of continuous economic progress.

Profit margin: It is marginal revenue minus marginal costs.

Purchasing power: A measure of the value of the medium of exchange in terms of the goods that can be purchased per unit of money.

Reciprocity: A relationship involving mutual exchange.

Risk: Due to uncertainty and imperfect knowledge there is a possibility of a loss.

Savings: It is the portion of income set aside for future consumption.

Scarcity: Available resources at any given moment are insufficient or inadequate relative to wants.

Shortage: This occurs when demand exceeds supply.

Speculating: It involves sophisticated guesswork about future changes that are shrouded in uncertainty; it is alertness in a risk environment.

Subjectivism: The scientific approach that recognizes that humans act subjectively, and this then leads to realistic and relevant scientific discoveries.

Subjectivist methodology: Using the science of human action to identify both laws and how they operate.

Standard of Living: An aggregate reference point assessing the degree of well-being and prosperity in relative terms.

Supply: The outcome of production.

Surplus: This occurs when supply exceeds demand.

Symmetry: When things are balanced and proportional.

Tautologies: These are propositions that are, in themselves, logically true.

Time Preference: The universal law of human action that states that people prefer to have a good now rather than that same good sometime in the future.

Unhampered Economy: A synonym for a laissez-faire economy and a free market economy. It is also the condition that exists in a divine economy.

Vantage Point Planes: The two dimensional surface, like a painter's canvas, seen from the perspective that is perpendicular to the plane.

Virtues: The human essence that is the origin of value, the source of wealth.

List of References

[1] A. ˉ. Ayer. The a priori. In Arthur Pap Paul Edwards, editor, *A Modern Introduction to Philosophy*, pages 646–57. Free Press, New York, 1965.

[2] Walter Block. *Defending the Undefendable: The Pimp, Prostitute, Scab, Slumlord, Libeler, Moneylender, and Other Scapegoats in the Rogue's Gallery of American Society*. Fox & Wilkes, San Francisco, 1991.

[3] F. A. Hayek. The use of knowledge in society. *The American Economic Review*, XXXV(4), September 1945.

[4] Linda Kavelin-Popov, Dan Popov, and John Kavelin. *The Family Virtues Guide: Simple Ways to Bring Out the Best in Our Children and Ourselves*. Penguin Books of Canada, Ltd., 1997.

[5] Israel M. Kirzner. *Competition & Entrepreneurship*. University of Chicago Press, Chicago, Phoenix edition, 1973.

[6] Bruce Koerber. *More Than Laissez-Faire*. Divine Economy. Invisible Order, 2015.

[7] Carl Menger. *Principles of Economics*. New York University Press, 1976.

[8] Murray N. Rothbard. *Man, Economy, and State*. Ludwig von Mises Institute, scholar's edition, 2004.

[9] Milton M. Shapiro. *Foundations of the Market Price System*. The Ludwig von Mises Institute, Auburn, Alabama, 2007.

[10] Thomas C. Taylor. *An Introduction to Austrian Economics*. The Ludwig von Mises Institute, 1983.

[11] Ludwig von Mises. *Money, Method and the Market Process*. Kluwer Academic Publishers, 1990.

[12] Ludwig von Mises. *Human Action*. Fox & Wilkes, San Francisco, fourth revised edition, 1996.

[13] Ludwig von Mises. *Epistemological Problems of Economics*. The Ludwig von Mises Institute, third edition, 2002.

About the Author

Bruce Koerber—the originator of the divine economy theory and the divine economy models.

The whole theory and the associated models developed as part of a deductive process. The simple model appeared to be organic and easily took on the characteristics inherent in the philosophy of classical liberalism. The first stage of its development ended with a dynamic macroeconomic model. Pursuing further the deductive process the model fit perfectly into a structural analysis that penetrated into the very heart of economic activity all the way to the origin of where value comes from. This discovery process yielded the microeconomic model.

Two major realms of the divine economy model remained unexplored. The first was the ethical strand which had to do with the connection between the human spirit expressed as purposeful human action, and transformation which is manifest in the capital structure. The perspective of the divine economy theory renewed macro and micro economics, granted, but the melding together of ethics and economics in theory and in a model had never been achieved before.

The last component of the divine economy model is just as earthshaking. This time the relationship between law and order brought to light the role of the equilibrium forces of the economy in the advancement of civilization by balancing all aspects of social cooperation, most notably liberty and justice.